MW00831369

PRAISE FOR *ATTUNED*

"Inspiring and informative, Thomas Hübl's *Attuned* takes us on a timely journey traversing the science of connection and the mystical explorations making the often-invisible threads of our lives—across time and space—visible to our everyday sight."

DANIEL J. SIEGEL, MD
New York Times bestselling author of
IntraConnected, Aware, and *Mind*

"Thomas Hübl invites us into a lived experience of interdependence . . . and helps us awaken the courage and wisdom needed to bring healing to our traumatized world."

TARA BRACH, PHD
author of *Radical Acceptance*
and *Trusting the Gold*

"*Attuned* is truly indispensable for those who seek to cultivate a deep and lasting connectivity with the paradox and complexity of their inner experience in such a way that they tap into the superpowers that every human has to heal themselves, their relationships, and, therefore, the world."

SARÁ KING, PHD
neuroscientist, CEO and founder
of MindHeart Consulting

"There is good medicine here, wise understandings and a vision for the transformation of heart and culture."

JACK KORNFIELD
author of *A Path With Heart*

"In this seminal work, Thomas Hübl goes beyond trauma as an individual wound to encompassing the relational and collective injury that must be addressed if we are truly able to heal the injuries to the collective psyche, to our relationships, to society, and, ultimately, to the world community. In his words: 'May we honor one another . . . and enrich the collective soil for the future flourishing of all sentient beings.' Please read, be enriched by this powerful work, and let each of us carry forth this healing in our own way."

PETER A. LEVINE, PHD
author of *Waking the Tiger*
and *In an Unspoken Voice*

"Thomas Hübl, a true visionary, has produced a must-read guide to relational intelligence and healing personal and generational trauma. A masterful achievement!"

DIANE POOLE HELLER, PHD
creator of DARe – Dynamic Attachment
Re-patterning experience, author of *The Power of Attachment* and *Healing Your Attachment Wounds*

"With the eloquence of a poet and the mind of a scientist, Thomas Hübl describes his mystical approach to transformation that has helped so many. His application of attuned awareness and resonance to traumatized relational fields offers new hope for the collective healing of large, influential systems, as well as individuals, that is inspiring."

RICHARD C. SCHWARTZ, PHD
creator of Internal Family Systems, author of
No Bad Parts and *You Are the One You've Been Waiting For*

"Thomas Hübl is not only a visionary but also the leader we so desperately need. Like an intimate conversation with a mystic of our modern era, Hübl's book invites you to contemplate your internal landscape as it relates to the world we share. Within these pages, you are invited to explore the interpersonal and transpersonal realms while simultaneously grounding yourself cellularly and energetically. This path of embodied spirituality recognizes that attuning to the subtle shifts that happen internally has the potential to expand the social fabric we share for the benefit of the collective. This is the book we have been waiting for."

ARIELLE SCHWARTZ, PHD
clinical psychologist, author of *The Complex PTSD Workbook* and *The Post-Traumatic Growth Guidebook*

"There's something rigorous, earnest, and heartbreakingly kind about Thomas Hübl's gentle approach to the matter of trauma and how we might address it today. This book is engorged with a beautiful generosity that's difficult to turn away from. Read it. Better yet, feel it."

BAYO AKOMOLAFE, PHD
author of *These Wilds Beyond Our Fences*

"In *Attuned*, Thomas Hübl brilliantly articulates the profound message that the essence of humanity is linked to an innate and universal need to connect with others and nature. In his book we are alerted to both the optimistic and positive consequences of listening to this message and the dire consequence of ignoring the signals that trigger our need to connect."

STEPHEN W. PORGES, PHD
Distinguished University Scientist at Indiana University, professor of psychiatry at University of North Carolina, author of *The Polyvagal Theory*

"Thomas Hübl does it again by writing another incisive text and inviting us to develop one of the most important evolutionary skills that we urgently need in this historical moment. This book claims that the practice of interdependence through different levels of attunement could awaken profound levels of healing and reinvigorate our commitment to our collective flourishing. I am broken open by this invitation."

ANGEL ACOSTA, EDD
principal consultant at Acosta Consulting

"We are ultimately not alone or separate. Consider the idea that everything we do affects the next seven generations, and realize that we have been affected by the past seven generations. This is just one of the reasons to embrace Thomas Hübl's new book, *Attuned*, where he offers pragmatic ways and methods to help heal trauma in this world. We can't do it alone, and it's never too late to start with this practical guide."

SHARON SALZBERG
author of *Lovingkindness* and *Real Life*

"Thomas Hübl does more than replace our current delusions of control and individualism with an enlightened paradigm of interconnectedness —he shows us how to live it, in our bodies, with those we love, in nature, with Spirit. *Attuned* offers a map and a practicable tool kit. It may be nothing less than the way forward beyond this mess we're all in, the urgent next step in our own evolutionary development. It is simply one of the most hopeful and important books I've read in decades."

TERRENCE REAL
New York Times bestselling author of *Us*

attuned

ALSO BY THOMAS HÜBL
with Julie Jordan Avritt

Healing Collective Trauma: A Process for Integrating
Our Intergenerational and Cultural Wounds

attuned

Practicing Interdependence to
Heal Our Trauma—and Our World

THOMAS HÜBL

with Julie Jordan Avritt

sounds true
BOULDER, COLORADO

Sounds True
Boulder, CO 80306

Some names and identifying details have been changed to protect the privacy of
individuals. This book is not intended as a substitute for the medical recommendations
of physicians, mental-health professionals, or other health-care providers. Rather,
it is intended to offer information to help the reader cooperate with physicians,
mental-health professionals, and health-care providers in a mutual quest for optimal
well-being. We advise readers to carefully review and understand the ideas presented
and to seek the advice of a qualified professional before attempting to use them.

Published 2023

Book design by Meredith Jarrett

Printed in Canada

BK06749

Library of Congress Cataloging-in-Publication Data
Names: Hübl, Thomas, author. | Jordan Avritt, Julie, author.
Title: Attuned : practicing interdependence to heal our trauma-and our
    world / Thomas Hübl with Julie Jordan Avritt.
Description: Boulder, CO : Sounds True, 2023. | Includes bibliographical
    references.
Identifiers: LCCN 2022058076 (print) | LCCN 2022058077 (ebook) | ISBN
    9781649631565 (hardcover) | ISBN 9781649631572 (ebook)
Subjects: LCSH: Psychic trauma--Social aspects. | Social psychology. |
    Cognitive psychology. | Subconsciousness.
Classification: LCC BF175.5.P75 H83 2023 (print) | LCC BF175.5.P75
    (ebook) | DDC 155.9/3--dc23/eng/20221208
LC record available at https://lccn.loc.gov/2022058076
LC ebook record available at https://lccn.loc.gov/2022058077

10 9 8 7 6 5 4 3 2 1

FSC
www.fsc.org
MIX
Paper from
responsible sources
FSC® C016245

To our humanity. May we honor one another and heal our relational wounds, enriching the collective soil for the future flourishing of all sentient beings.

And to my beloved wife, Yehudit, and daughter, Eliya, whose love and generosity support my work at its base.

Contents

Introduction   1

Part One

1. Ancient Principles, Evolutionary Insights   11
   Practice: Mapping the Inner-Body Landscape   23

2. Essential Principles of Human Development   27
   Practice: Stress Assessment and Reduction   43

3. The Art of Attunement   45
   Practice: Inner-Body Attunement   48
   Practice: The Three-Sync Technique   58

4. The Art of Transparent Communication   63
   Practice: Relational Attunement   76

5. Presencing the Shadow   79
   Practice: Processing the Karma of the Day   89

6. Trauma's Impact   95

Part Two

7. The Power of Healing Relation   115

8. Guidance for Facilitators of Healing   131

9. Ancestral Healing   159
   Practice: A Simple Ancestral Healing   176

10. Healing for the Collective   179
    Practice: Global Social Witnessing   187

   Epilogue   199

   Acknowledgments   203
   Notes   205
   Resources   215
   About the Author   219
   About the Co-author   221

Introduction

This is a dark time, filled with suffering and uncertainty. Like living cells in a larger body, it is natural that we feel the trauma of our world. So, don't be afraid of the anguish you feel, or the anger or fear, because these responses arise from the depth of your caring and the truth of your interconnectedness with all beings.

—JOANNA MACY AND SAM MOWE

We live in stark times. Across the world, nations are colored by intensifying rancor and hostility. A sharp tableau of deepening division and civic unrest rises against a backdrop of mounting political authoritarianism. Even long-standing democracies are proving vulnerable to threat or dissolution. Political, racial, ethnic, religious, and sectarian conflicts are waged again or anew, while global arms traders, regional drug cartels, and every platform for local and international organized crime continue to profit. War refugees, climate migrants, and weary travelers of all stripes face outright persecution and hidden indignities. In many places, the poor grow poorer, while indigenous peoples experience continued suppression and denigration, if not protracted extermination. Tribal lands are newly stolen, occupied, or spoiled; ancient rites are desecrated and lifeways dishonored; and ancestors are disrespected or forgotten—all while our planet's life-giving forests burn unmitigated and its rivers and oceans grow steadily more toxic. Traumatized persons haunt traumatized landscapes.

Yet, however dire, these realities need not be read as signs of certain apocalypse. We belong to a living planetary system—a living, thriving cosmos—that is self-organizing and self-healing. Humans are not apart from nature; we are *of* nature. Regardless of humanity's current condition, we are never truly separate or even solely individual; we are members of a radical, co-evolving whole. Pearls in Indra's net, we belong to and arise from the "great distributive lattice,"[1] the elegant, cosmic web of causal interdependence.

Consider these things: the impossibly delicate watermeal, a flowering aquatic plant smaller than a grain of rice, is rootless and free floating. Yet, it can locate and connect with just one or even thousands of its own kind, as well as with tiny plants of other species, to form life-sustaining mats across the surface of a placid duck pond. And this: the simple, humble mushroom, which sends its delicate fibers (mycelium) deep into the ground in a widely arcing radius. By casting a net from these tiny probing filaments, the fungus links itself to the roots of nearby plants, trees, and other fungi—and in the process connects each to the others. This organic "internet" produces a symbiotic mechanism for communication, water location, nutrient exchange, and mutual defense against infection, infestation, and disease. The presence of fungal mycelia allows nearby trees to communicate across distances, alerting other trees, even those of different species, to the presence of invading insects, thereby signaling the production of biochemical-repellent defenses. Almost magically, trees use mycelia to transfer essential nitrogen, carbon, and phosphorous, sustaining the life and health of not only those trees but the entire local ecosystem of plants, insects, animals, and even humans.

Perhaps more astonishingly, fungal mycelia have proven to be cheap, abundant, and powerful natural remediators of many types of toxins left behind in soil and wastewater: heavy metals, petroleum fuels, pesticides, herbicides, pharmaceuticals, personal-care products, dyes, and even plastics.[2] Fungal mycelia naturally break down offending pollutants, creating cleaner, safer, *healthier* land and water.

If a life-form the size of a pinhead (the watermeal) or one seemingly as simple as a mushroom can reach out to other species to do any or all of these things—self-organize, connect, communicate, assist, protect, defend, heal, and *restore*—why couldn't humans? After all, we, too, belong to nature. Perhaps each of these qualities (and many more) are imbued in us—inbuilt characteristics of what it means to be alive on this particular planet, orbiting this particular star, in this particular galaxy. Perhaps intelligent interdependence is our natural, even sacred, endowment, one we can lean into, enhance, and strengthen in service of our own species, and all others.

After all, the refusal to honor our interdependence and enact healthy and sustained relations has caused no end of suffering. If the underlying challenge of climate change (or any other wicked or systemic social problem) can be traced to human disrelation—a state of being *out of accordance* with nature, ourselves, and other humans—then I propose it to be a fundamentally *spiritual* problem, as much as an environmental, scientific, technological, cultural, psychological, economic, or historical one. To construct an adequate or sufficiently innovative response to the challenge, we must think holistically. It is time to bridge East and West, to marry the wisdom of our ancient and long-standing spiritual traditions to the revelations of contemporary science. As we bring the power of scientific insight to bear on our understanding of modern social ills, we may amplify our capacity to integrate that information with the rich awakening practices of consciousness offered by our world's mystical traditions. In this way, we may awaken to and further develop our most intrinsic biological gifts: the powers to self-organize, connect, communicate, assist, protect, defend, heal, and restore.

And more.

Perhaps, instead of finding ourselves alive in a time of exponential, unstoppable decline, we will discover the power to awaken and initiate newer, higher, evolutionary gifts. Though, to accomplish any or all of these things, I believe we must do them together—not separately, but in relation.

In her 1997 book, *God's Ecstasy: The Creation of a Self-Creating World,* mathematician, philosopher, and contemplative theologian Beatrice Bruteau described the divine order of the cosmos—what she saw as the original imprint of creation, as an expression of "symbiotic unity"[3] (a pattern observed in our fungal mycelia). Author, theologian, and Episcopal priest Cynthia Bourgeault has termed this quality "holographic reciprocity," where "the whole and the part exist in an interabiding unity." The whole, Bourgeault writes, is "not a substance, but a *field of action*," generated by the dynamic and ceaseless exchange of what Catalan Catholic priest and interfaith advocate Raimon Panikkar describes as "pure relationality."[4]

In the twelfth century, Hildegard of Bingen, the German Benedictine abbess and mystic visionary wrote: "O Holy Spirit, you are the mighty way in which everything that is in the heavens, on the earth, and under the earth, is penetrated with connectedness, penetrated with relatedness."[5] More than eight centuries later, Thomas Berry captured the same: "The universe is a communion of subjects, rather than a collection of objects."[6]

These thinkers articulated a profoundly mystical vision of the nature of reality. When taken together with the intimately relational nature of the quantum universe, or as the late theoretical physicist John Wheeler termed it, the "participatory universe," we arrive at fundamentally compatible ontologies.

Brigid Brophy, the novelist and social reformer, wrote in 1968 about the strange and incomparable genius of nineteenth-century English illustrator, Aubrey Beardsley. Remarking on Beardsley's unique talent, Brophy wrote: ". . . he is dramatizing not the relationships between personalities, but the pure, geometric essence of relationship."[7] And that is our aim, precisely: *the pure, geometric essence of relationship.*

Like the most refined alchemical distillate or some primary source code, the architecture of true human connection somehow includes yet transcends the personal; interdependence is at once deeply intimate and utterly universal. Pure moments of relating reach us at the root, touching who we truly are, while simultaneously elevating what it is possible for us to become. The sacred geometry of active interrelation is both a portal to everything we have ever been, individually and ancestrally, and a gateway to the greater future potential of our species. To colocate this future experientially is a sacred act of communion and a natural rite of "symbiotic unity."

These things should not be taken as Pollyanna-ish ideals. To arrive even at the furthest glimmer of the distant edge of our becoming, we have crossed an historic dark night. We have come face to face with the abyss, and in it, we must now reckon with the possibility of our own extinction. To survive, much less to flourish, we must make conscious our essential interdependence and awaken into new forms of vibrant, sustained relation.

I have taken on a vocation around spiritual practice, dedicating my life and work to what I call the *inner science of consciousness*. The territory of consciousness can be explored and understood through practices like meditation, study, prayer, movement, stillness, and through contemplation of self and nature—as well as in contemplation of the relational dynamics that exist between ourselves and others in the ordinary course of modern life (or what I call the *marketplace*). In my years of personal practice and professional facilitation, I have seen the many and profound ways that such practices grow and evolve us, enriching our lives and enlivening our understanding. And it is the translucing power of relational practices to transform us that has captivated me most.

In part I of this book, I propose a core, awareness-based practice, one I call *transparent communication*. This practice is not just intended to improve our communications skills, though it does that. As a contemplative exercise, transparent communication is designed to bring us deeper into pure relationality. As a practical tool, the work enlarges our sense of relation to self, coheres our sense of connection to and belonging with others, and enhances the ways we exist in family and community. It can even advance the ways we participate in and co-create culture by bringing us into a higher level of social awareness and engagement, which is the foundation for resilient democracies. Indeed, the purpose of transparent communication is to deepen our relationship to life itself.

In part II of this book, we will apply the essentials of transparent communication to the therapeutic context for individual, ancestral, and collective healing. Transparent communication is not a standalone practice exclusive to one-to-one relationships, but it is at the heart of conscious relating—with ourselves, in our families, with our ancestors, and with one another in ever larger groups.

In the more challenging moments of modern life, our sense of awareness often becomes constricted and limited. In times of difficulty and stress, we tend to lose perception of the greater field as our awareness clusters tightly within us. We become compactly self-focused by default. As a result, we are less available; we lose access to those resources that allow us to feel with and for others. Whether we're in the middle of difficult family or relationship disagreements or embroiled in the heat of workplace conflict, a sense of separation becomes heightened, and it is difficult to be present. This is not wrong; it is simply an evolutionary function that promotes survival—an adaptation to biological utility.

Deep in our nervous systems, we carry these ancient survival patterns, most of which are millions of years old, borne to us by our mammalian forebears. By contrast, transparent communication offers an evolutionary opening in consciousness. It arrives alongside similar practices at a time of deep global division and struggle, offering us tools for better navigating difficulty, enhancing our availability to be present, and expanding our awareness to include the space, energy, and subtle structures operating within and around us.

This *relational field* is a vast matrix of energy—information in motion—which exists within, around, and between us. Transparent communication helps us to bear witness to this field. It is about *relating* more than it is about relationship. It is a verb, not a noun; a process, not a thing. The more we practice, the more our awareness grows so that we begin to observe and distinguish not only aspects of the relational field that are fluid and clear but also those that are rigid, frozen, stuck, dissociated, and in shadow. And we learn to perceive the impact of individual and collective trauma upon the field. The effect of transparent communication is the power to illuminate that field, infusing its byways and interstices with the light and lucidity of awareness, to bring healing and repair to the collective.

When I speak to groups or before an audience at an event, it is not enough that I show up knowing what I wish to say. To be effective, I must be in dialogue with the whole and, therefore, aware of the group or the audience as a dynamic system. Only noticing what is happening for me is not enough; I must be able to accurately feel and adapt to the needs of my listeners. I need to clearly sense my participants' degree of availability and curiosity. I also need to perceive whether and when I am being heard and received—or what else might be needed or present. The clarifying of the relational matrix comes with expanded awareness and offers an acceleration of our coming-into-relation. This is the leading edge of communication and leadership, and it requires deeper awareness of the intersubjective space from all.

Throughout this book, you will find an exploration of mystical and scientific theory alongside opportunities for guided contemplation. A committed practice to any artistic or other endeavor eventually delivers competence, perhaps even excellence. As an engaged contemplative practice, the art of transparent communication is no different. Dedication rewards mastery.

We can shape our daily lives into a deep and steady practice for accessing higher relational skills, working toward mastery in our ability to:

- embrace the qualities of stillness and movement

- recognize the functions and forms of perception

- transcend outmoded habits

- illuminate the relational field, filling it with awareness

- learn the arts of attunement, sensing, and presencing

Facing the complexity, uncertainty, volatility, and ambiguity of our time with wisdom requires our coming into clearer alignment, deeper coherence, and truer connection—with ourselves and one another, with nature, and with the cosmos. To prepare the way, we must study and practice. I offer this book in service of the path.

part one

In part I of this book, we will explore the mystical principles behind human development and human connection: how each soul embodies and grows through the expression of the will and with the support of present and attuned caregivers and loved ones. This growth is led ever forward by the universal drives of being and becoming, autonomy and belonging—the ballast and the sail—which offers both stability and direction. At the center of these is the fulcrum of relationship: nearly everything in the human story depends on the quality of our connections to one another.

So, in a book about attunement, connection, and awakened interdependence, we must necessarily confront the sand in the engine, the inhibitory effect of unwitnessed, unhealed trauma on development and its fracturing impact on our capacity to relate with self and others. Yet, as they say, the medicine is in the wound. Though trauma disrupts the act of relation, conscious attunement can help us create internal and external coherence, consciously regulate the nervous system, process toxic stress, and feel more embodied and more connected with others. Attunement practices are healing tools for dealing with the effects of trauma—whether in people or across communities—and transparent communication is one such practice.

1

Ancient Principles, Evolutionary Insights

*The universe and the observer exist as a pair. I cannot imagine
a consistent theory of the universe that ignores consciousness.*

—ANDREI LINDE

*Care of the soul begins with observance of how the
soul manifests itself and how it operates.*

—THOMAS MOORE

amed physicist John Wheeler once said: "No phenomenon
is a real phenomenon unless it is an observed phenomenon."[1]
He wasn't being cheeky; he meant it literally. Wheeler's strange
observation was not immediately greeted with universal applause, of
course. Truly radical ideas are often difficult to grok, and one prevailing
order takes time to give way to the next.

In classical physics, objects exist. Planets, asteroids, and molecules
have established properties and discernable characteristics, and they generally do as expected. If a classical tree falls in a forest and no one is there
to hear it, the tree doesn't care; it produces a riot of sound waves when
it hits the ground. But in the strange world of quantum mechanics, our

"tree" is a subatomic particle, and paradoxically *a particle is a wave is a particle.* The particle/wave exists everywhere and nowhere at once, so to speak, as a probabilistic phenomenon. Stranger still, a quantum tree only pops into existence as a discrete entity with discernable characteristics, a location, and behavior when there is someone to observe its efforts—i.e., it does not even *show up* in the forest until someone is present to hear it fall.

According to the new quantum story (as described by John Wheeler), consciousness is required for anything much to happen at all. Strange, indeed. "The farther we peer into space," writes scientist Robert Lanza, "the more we realize that the nature of the universe cannot be understood fully by inspecting spiral galaxies or watching distant supernovas. It lies deeper. It involves our very selves."[2]

After the Enlightenment got going (i.e., somewhere between the lifetimes of René Descartes and Werner Heisenberg), physicists and most otherwise rational people accepted what has become the prevailing belief: namely, that ours is an objective universe, material and insensate, existing "out there." Somehow, experts surmised, the great big physical cosmos banged into existence and lumbered along more or less steadily for billions of years before anything like the trilobite or triceratops or wolf or human called it home. This is the general cosmological story that is now largely taken for granted.

In five vastly abridged steps, that story goes more or less like so:

1. First, by some unknowable accident, *stuff* showed up—such as stars and gases and rocks and minerals and mountains.

2. Much later, and likewise inexplicably, *life* appeared. Initially, life was terribly simple, though nonetheless strange, given the otherwise inanimate order of things.

3. By and by, life inadvertently complexified by way of many random mutations. It learned to consume sunlight and laid down a green carpet across the planet—mosses, ferns, flowers, trees, etcetera.

4. Still later, after life had accomplished a *lot* more mutating, it managed to grow profoundly more complex, á la the nervous system, vertebrae, feathers, fur, and so on. And, whether simple or complex, life's overriding objective was to survive long enough to successfully reproduce and thereby propagate its genes, for posterity.

5. All of this continued apace until life complexified again and—*boom!*—was suddenly walking around on two legs, playing with fire, planting crops, waging war, building city-states, and inflicting upon itself intricate religious practices (again, for posterity). Before you knew it, life had circumnavigated the globe; laid down rail lines and highways; sent probes into outer space; and devised, erected, and surfed the internet! Even now, life is busy cooking up recipes for *artificial* life.

It is, of course, impossible to capture this incredible cosmology in so few words. Suffice it to say that, just as humankind began to understand the material universe—the world of bodies and planets and bowling balls—and its sweeping evolutionary processes, another radical recognition about the nature of pretty much everything began to dawn.

Every epoch has its Copernicus, its Galileo: someone rascally enough to pick up the book *This Is What We Know Absolutely to Be True* and pitch it directly in the nearest bonfire (or at the very least, commence the writing of a bold new chapter). So it was in 1927, when two American physicists, Clinton Davisson and Lester Germer, shook the prevailing scientific paradigm. With their now famous double-slit experiment, Davisson and Germer provably demonstrated the importance of an observer (or, if you will, consciousness) on the state of things. Their experiment repeatedly demonstrated that, whenever someone pays attention as a subatomic particle or a quantum of light is fired in the direction of two parallel slits, the particle does precisely what you would expect. It appears to pass through one slit or the other and hits the surface or wall behind, just like an ordinary bullet or a baseball. But if no one is watching as the particle is fired, it behaves like a wave, representing all probabilities and mysteriously passing through both slits at once.

By the late twentieth century, another paradigm rattler, who worked at the University of Geneva, flipped the story still further, forever upending what we collectively call reality. In 1997, physicist Nicolas Gisin successfully pulled off a radical experiment, proving a theory not even Einstein had been able to wrap his head around. In his experiments, Gisin was able to separate two entangled photons (light particles) by a distance of seven miles, sending each in the opposite direction along an optical fiber. When one of the pair of photons hit a two-way mirror, particle detectors recorded whether it randomly went through the mirror or bounced off. The world-shattering part: whichever action the proton took, its entangled twin simultaneously made the precise complimentary action—seven miles away. Spookily, it was as if these entangled photons had instantaneously communicated with one another from a distance.[3] Now, it is not necessarily true that a message "traveled" from here to there, faster than the speed of light. It is more that Newtonian spatial separation (conditions in the macro realm) does not appear to impede quantum relationality (conditions in the micro realm).

In the years since, Gisin's experiment has been successfully replicated, proving one of the weirder theories to emerge out of quantum mechanics. Its central revelation: whether entangled particles are separated by seven miles or the length of multiple galaxies, they are never truly separate. In fact, Gisin and others now believe the quantum communication occurring in entanglement may also be present in objects at the macroscopic scale,[4] potentially even those visible to the naked eye.

Nature and consciousness are correlative, interdependent, *relational*. And the observer is fundamentally entangled with the universe it witnesses.

In the quantum era, we are collectively arriving at an altogether strange realization, though one that Gautama Buddha surmised some 2,400 years ago: so much about the nature of reality depends upon consciousness. Nature and consciousness are correlative, interdependent, *relational.* And the observer is fundamentally entangled with the universe it witnesses.

It stands to reason, then, that if we have any hope of building a better world, we should turn our attention to the essence of the observer and take a look at consciousness itself. What follows is an exploration into the mystical principles undergirding the arresting insights of quantum science, principles that have been with us for millennia.

THE MYSTICAL PRINCIPLES

Throughout time and across cultures, the world's great mystical traditions have pointed again and again to a set of core, universal insights. Whether studying the yogic traditions of Hinduism, the Sufism of mystical Islam, Vajrayana and other forms of Buddhism, the Kabbalistic schools of Judaism, or the contemplative traditions of mystical Christianity, one encounters a recurring set of essential truths. Among these are principles describing the central-most qualities of existence: stillness, movement, and awareness.

The principle of stillness can be found through the quieting of the mind. When we practice stillness, a deep feeling of interior spaciousness can arise. Spaciousness is the first level of stillness. With spaciousness, we can drop into the depths of unformed stillness, causal awareness, emptiness, "thusness," or the void.

Connecting to greater stillness expands your sense of availability and affords a deeper, more wakeful feeling of presence. With practice, the experience of stillness, spaciousness, and presence deepens, allowing you to witness your daily process with awareness. All contemplative practices are a guide for increasing one's awareness, as so much exists that is hidden or out of the range of ordinary perception.

In yoga, the asana of *Savasana*, or Corpse Pose, is at base a stillness practice. Lying prone at the end of their postures, yoga practitioners focus simply on quieting the body and mind, consciously relaxing one muscle group after another. A sense of peace washes over the practitioner as the mind and body learn to let go, to be still. This stillness practice reduces stress, enhances spaciousness, and fosters a sense of well-being.

When life is consistently busy and stressful or when you are running from task to task, dealing with one objective or problem after the next, you can easily burn out. Your system overloads as your inner resources are depleted. Living life this way is unsustainable; humans need time and space to relax, repair, and regenerate the body and mind—to recharge the batteries, so to speak. Making regular time to reflect on your experiences and to decompress and restore your energies allows you to digest the content of your life so that when you return to it, you can be more effective, more present, more at peace.

Again, a stillness practice increases your sense of inner space. And the degree of inner spaciousness you experience is directly correlated to your capacity to handle complexity. What the late Oliver Wendell Holmes, Jr., called the "simplicity on the other side of complexity"[5] refers beautifully to this notion. Without sufficient space, however, complexity can overwhelm you, which creates a feeling of contraction. Your ability to adapt to complexity depends on your facility for inner space and witness, as well as on having the right cup: the inner structure or container through which to hold and process new information.

Through meditation, you can discover that in fact you *are* space. You learn to attune to the stillness you inhabit, to enhance the spaciousness you occupy, and to listen deeply from this place to your interior and exterior environment, to both yourself and others. With greater connection to stillness, you have more availability, more "room" as a base from which to presence your world. You can tune in and listen more fully, connect more deeply. Greater availability allows you not only to absorb what I share with you, but to *host* me within you. Of course, when you feel overwhelmed by the demands of life, your sense of stillness, spaciousness, and availability become reduced or absent, and your capacity to host another is compromised. You can no longer be fully present for other people. For these reasons, the ability to connect with stillness is a key ingredient for relationality.

Whether you are in a business meeting, a casual encounter with an acquaintance, or a deep family discussion, you can sense how available another person is to you. Availability is a foundation of *response*-ability; one requires the first to accomplish the second. Your capacity to respond to another from your authentic core depends on your level of availability. When you are stressed or contracted by overwhelm, you will be less available, less able to respond to others from your core. Stress generates reactivity rather than responsiveness. In significant stress, you may feel cornered, threatened, taxed. You feel other people are demanding "too much" or that you lack the resources to respond to their needs. In stress, you feel there is never enough space or time.

Whether managing professional work, connecting with family and friends, making love to an intimate partner, or spending time with children, your capacity to show up fully is dependent on the quality of inner space—and, therefore, inner availability—that you bring. Think about it: when you feel fully present and available for your children, an immediate intimacy is created. You experience a deep quality of connectedness, and your children seem to blossom in your presence. When you have less availability, however, your children suffer—as do you.

Given the incredible pace of modern life and the sheer amount of information we encounter each day, it is all too easy to discover—often after the fact—that we lack adequate availability for our colleagues, our partners, and our children. With dozens of daily emails, calls, and text notifications demanding our attention, it is all the more important to practice stillness. We feel almost claustrophobic, as though we are pressed against glass; there isn't enough *space*. If we find ourselves in a disagreement with an intimate partner or close colleague, we feel further constricted. The space within us feels reduced or disappeared. We might even hear ourselves say, "I don't have time for this!"

But when we find someone who is fully available to listen, fully present with us, it feels so good. Their presence alone seems to inject more spaciousness into our experience. When another person is truly available in this way, they are able to bring their full intelligence to the interaction; then the space between us—the intersubjective space— becomes healing ground.

In the Jewish tradition, Shabbat is honored for the biblical seventh day, which according to the Book of Genesis, the Creator took for rest. Shabbat represents the sacredness of stillness and, therefore, of space, availability, and presence of being. And it points us toward the quiet mindfulness that allows us to honor and nurture these qualities in ourselves. As we practice, we discover that these resources are, in fact, ever abundant. Stillness is timeless. And space, like time, is boundless.

If stillness is being, movement is becoming. Out of causal stillness, everything arises—and fundamentally, every "thing" in our cosmos is energy. Movement, therefore, is the flow of energy, information, and creativity. It is the motion of light, heat, electricity, magnetism, gravity, and all processes of life and matter. It is emotion, thought, belief, inspiration, innovation, and creativity. Energy is intelligence in action; life is movement.

Energy is intelligence in action; life is movement.

Whether we call it information, data, intelligence, vitality, or energy, life seeks always to express itself: to move and flow as a river must move and flow. When we become overwhelmed by the demands of our lives, we tend to perceive our stress as a by-product of some insufficiency—a lack of time, support, rest, or other resource. Next to this perceived insufficiency, our responsibilities feel like too much. Yet, from a mystical understanding, this sense of "too much" is simply about friction.

Friction occurs whenever resistance is met between a given structure and the flow of energy or other resources. Imagine the pipes that bring water into your home. If the pipes are too narrow for the water pressure or if they become clogged, there's a problem. We can say that the structure is inadequate for the channel of energy (in this case, water). Adjustments in water pressure or repairs to the pipes must be made to set everything right again.

When energetic intelligence becomes stuck or blocked anywhere in the body, vital life force is inhibited and a sense of tension and pressure are created. Initially, we experience this as stress or discomfort, but eventually it can become illness or disease. Some blocks are significant enough to delay development and inhibit potential, which leads to the suppression of one's purpose. These effects will be felt in the body—and also in the emotions and thoughts.

The human soul expresses both stillness and movement; it is the nature of the soul to be and to become. These expressions of soul belong to what I refer to as the *three innate and inalienable human rights*: the right of being, the right of becoming (the unfolding of potential), and the right of belonging (the right to build healthy relational bonds and to experience oneself as part of a community). When these fundamental expressions of the soul are ignored or dishonored, relational bonds dissolve and human systems, whether families or governments, break down.

The object of transparent communication is to restore these expressions of the soul and repair human connection. As we practice transparent communication, we develop the capacity to sense and expand inner spaciousness, presence, and availability and to honor the rights of being, becoming, and belonging.

The practice of transparent communication brings us more deeply in touch with what is exterior to us, the people and circumstances of our environment, as well as with what is interior to us. With care and practice, we learn to cohere the perception that moves outward into the environment with the awareness that moves inward, into us. We may even learn to more clearly and adeptly "presence" what exists inside another. To communicate—to *co*-mmune—is to join my stream with your stream. Transparent communication brings shared witness to our communal stream so that we experience our mutuality with greater clarity.

As I learn to feel and inhabit my life more fully and to witness the flow of my emotions, my thoughts, my bodily senses and perceptions, and my past and present, I am better able to feel *with* and *for* you and others. Whatever lies latent or hidden within me becomes more transparent, more available, more present. My capacity for empathy deepens, and my relational awareness expands so that I begin to feel the living contours of interconnectedness, our interrelation. As philosopher, linguist, and poet Jean Gebser wisely wrote: "Our concern is to render transparent everything latent 'behind' and 'before' the world—to render transparent our origin, our entire human past, as well as the present, which already contains the future."[6]

FROM RIGIDITY TO FLOW

Another essential mystical principle to consider is that of habit. Habit is the organization of energy (i.e., the movement of data or intelligence), so that it becomes coded knowledge and is, therefore, always accessible, even automatic. Through the repeated "wiring" or reconstitution of energy patterns, *habits become structures*. Imagine if every morning you woke up and had to relearn how to walk or speak or drive! Unless neural structures become damaged, these skills are automatic, habitual.

Through hundreds of thousands of years of evolution, human beings have acquired all sorts of useful habits. In moments of real or perceived danger, the body produces precise chemical and hormonal outputs so that, without having to think about it, the body responds to threat: we flee danger or fight off attack. We do not have to learn to do this as children, just as we do not have to learn to feel attraction or desire for a mate; we simply do. When all is going reasonably well, the human body desires to seek out food and water, to reproduce, and to avoid pain and danger by seeking safety and connection. These are hardwired evolutionary structures or habits.

Of course, not all habits come naturally; many are learned. Some are culturally conditioned, while others emerge from the demands of contemporary life. The infinitely varied ways that we address one another, whether and how we worship, or how we interact in countless culturally informed scenarios take a little more thinking and learning, but these eventually become habits too. Of course, many of our personal or social habits become so structurally fixed that it can be difficult to upgrade them when new information indicates that we should. Although habituated structure frees up the energy we need for thinking, learning, and dealing with new problems, it can also prevent us from accessing the energy we need to address change.

The gift of an engaged contemplative practice is that, through enhancing spaciousness, availability, and presence, we can become mindful of even our most entrenched habits. We can determine with intelligence which structures are useful to us and which would benefit from a bit of remodeling. When everything in our lives flows automatically and according to habit, we tend to miss or ignore all the cues pointing to a need for change until we find ourselves confronted with crisis.

Every one of us knows how difficult it can be to alter even one habit. The energy of the habit has become crystallized, wired by the brain, and laid down firmly as a physical, mental, and even emotional pathway. If you want to bend a rigid structure such as a rod of metal, you need to heat it up (i.e., apply rapid-moving energy). Similarly, when you want to soften a fixed habit, you need to flood it with new energy and awareness. This creates more space for presence and mindfulness. We notice more, and this witnessing is a subtle form of intervention. As engaged witnesses, we are more attuned to the changes happening around and within us and are more available for the shifts occurring in an intimate partnership or within a child. We begin to sense finer qualities and subtler details or transitions that we may otherwise have missed.

Habits are essential to our lives and are even useful for our survival, but without noticing, we can become calcified, rigid, resistant to change, and, therefore, not resilient in the face of it. However, with awareness and presence, we can better move from rigidity into flow, recognizing when new energy is needed and adapting outmoded habits to embrace change.

It's wise to engage practices that help us to do so. For instance, famed quantum physicist Werner Heisenberg liked to take walks after working too long at his desk or in the lab. During those walks, he did his best thinking, and sudden inspiration often came to him. Writers William Wordsworth, Virginia Woolf, Charles Dickens, C. S. Lewis, and Henry David Thoreau were all walkers. Aristotle, Einstein, and Salvador Dalí found inspiration during naps. Countless other artists and geniuses prefer gardening, sailing, knitting, cooking, meditating, or simply taking a hot shower. What all these have in common is that they tend to expand one's sense of space. With more space comes more availability and presence so that inspiration and light (conscious and embodied awareness) can flow in.

When we are bent to a given task for too long, however, a feeling of tension and pressure eventually starts to build. We need to move or rest or otherwise shake ourselves loose from our efforts. Taking time to recharge is essential so that new energy, higher inspiration, and fresh creativity can enter again. Only from an open space of renewal can we access *emergence*, or future-flow—the flow of new potentials and new futures. Without rest, we are left to draw from habit and the structures of the past.

When we live any area of our lives too habitually or unconsciously—perhaps we find ourselves repeating negative relationship patterns, or simply denying our deepest purpose and calling—energetic blocks form, and we eventually feel discomfort. This is the result of *evolutionary* pressure: our habits and structures have become too narrow for the light seeking to flow through us. On some level, we can always sense the need for change. We know prolonged resistance is an invitation to crisis, wherein the "pipes" will burst and we will break open. If we listen to the evolutionary tension, however, we can use it to inform a path of growth. Often, the tension is telling us to release our habits for a moment and lean into the unknown, the new, the liminal edge where emergence arises.

As we connect to that edge-place, there is often a feeling of light pouring in. We have all felt this sometime in life, perhaps during a healing therapy session the moment that a vital breakthrough is reached. Suddenly, we see everything differently, with new wisdom and wonder. Perhaps during a difficult conversation or a moment of conflict, some new quality of understanding is touched, and it feels as if there is suddenly more space in the room through which grace and peace and light can enter. Or, after working long and hard to solve an intractable problem, we feel a sudden "*aha!*" The proverbial light bulb switches on, illuminating us with new insight and energy. In these moments, there is an upgrade in the capacity to witness—an elevation of awareness.

Conversely, when I am stressed or shut down—distracted, disconnected, and dissociated—I have less space and a reduced capacity for inner witness. In that state of contraction, I am more likely to become over-identified with my thoughts and emotions (habits) or constricted by the sensation of physical pain or discomfort. It becomes difficult to listen and communicate or solve problems. I feel "too busy" rather than productive; reactive rather than responsive. I function out of crystalized habits (according to my past) rather than creatively (according to my potential).

PRACTICE: MAPPING THE INNER-BODY LANDSCAPE

When asked, "How do you feel?" we may habitually respond without pausing to reflect or observe. "I'm fine," we might say, whether or not we truly feel fine. There is frequently a lack of coherence between what is felt by the body and what is being experienced emotionally or mentally. When we become aware of this incoherence, we start to notice our own areas of physical discomfort, tension, or dissociation. Likewise, we can sense incoherence in others. For example, you might notice when another person doesn't feel in touch with their body, as though they're not fully present in their physical form.

To create greater space, presence, and, therefore, coherence in our bodies, we can engage in a simple, contemplative technique. In this practice, you will witness your body from the inside by tuning in to its energies and sensations. While reading this, take a survey of your body, noticing the parts that feel more present and accessible. In these areas, you may notice there is more available information or aliveness.

Next, see whether you can observe which areas of the body feel less accessible or less available. Notice the contrast between the areas of your body that feel more alive and immediate and any areas where you may need to concentrate harder in order to feel. What happens when you move your awareness into these less available parts? What images, thoughts, or emotions come up?

After feeling the parts of your body that are open and accessible, see if you can check in with your current level of stress. Where does your stress currently fall on a scale from one to ten? Now notice the sensations you call "stress" and see if you can embrace those sensations a bit more, softening into the stress. See if you can hold an awareness of your bodily sensations *and* the stress, which will allow your nervous system to integrate some of the stress and redistribute that energy into the body's overall flow and relaxation.

Map your body's inner landscape daily, regularly observing its sensations and any other information it contains. With regular practice, you will notice a greater sense of coherence between your physical, emotional, and mental bodies. You will also be better able to witness—to feel *with*—what is happening inside another person.

An internal conflict or a polarization of emotions, beliefs, or ideas cannot be solved from the level of restriction (i.e., from the extremes). What's needed is more space to feel and, as a result, to witness the conflict to resolve these energies. In healing work, the inner world of the therapist, facilitator, or healer is an offering of space for the client's inner world, thereby increasing the space of awareness. Inner space is essential in any transformation process.

The practice of transparent communication is a dialectic—a way of being together in clarity with whatever is present. With practice and awareness, we can achieve a sense of balance between stillness and movement. We can attend to our habits, consciously adapting and changing the quality of our mental, emotional, and physical structures. It is a deepening of the I and the We, and it is a realization of our intrinsic interdependence.

The Kabbalists say that as you walk through life, you can perceive life only to the degree that you possess a clear instrument. Without the telescope, modern astronomy would not exist. Likewise, without the electron microscope, quantum physics as we know it might never have emerged. The practice of transparent communication is fundamentally about clarifying our instrument so that we can learn to perceive even the subtlest qualities with higher and higher resolution. The human body-mind complex, including the emotional layer, is our instrument, and it houses the potential for many refined structures and capacities of perception. Among these is the nervous system, a biological and energetic web of startling complexity and wisdom. In the next chapter, we will discuss the human nervous system in more depth, but suffice it to say there is much more to it than we understand on a typical physiological level. The nervous system connects us to a complete record, a vast inner library containing all of one's experiences across a lifetime. In fact, the human nervous system *connects us to one another*. Through transparent communication practices, we will learn to employ this evolutionary tool for deeper relational intelligence.

Another Kabbalist teaching is that of *tikkun*, meaning "repair of the world"[7] or "divine repair." Many Kabbalists concern themselves with the repair or healing of both individuals and the world. Transparent communication is a tool for tikkun, and we will learn to utilize it as much as an individual life practice as a resource for collective wisdom, healing, and integration.

To do that, we need to have a foundational understanding of trauma from both a mystical and a physiological perspective, along with how and why trauma disrupts development and harms communication. We'll begin by looking at the fundamental processes of human development, which we'll discuss in the next chapter.

2

Essential Principles of
Human Development

When anything really new begins to germinate around us, we
cannot distinguish it—for the very good reason that it could
only be recognized in the light of what is going to be.
—PIERRE TEILHARD DE CHARDIN

To understand trauma's impact on our development and relationships, we need to first look at the mystical and contemporary scientific explanations for how humans grow, mature, and connect—a process that begins at incarnation.

From the mystical perspective, we might say that light itself incarnates. What we perceive as light is itself an emission of energy and intelligence—of curiosity, longing, and desire or will. We could call this light the "evolutionary impulse," which was first used by French-Austrian psychologist Paul Diel. Here, we will refer to "light" simply as the human soul.

When the light of the human soul arrives in its present incarnation, it will have traveled through layer upon layer upon layer of time: hundreds of thousands of years of human history and *billions* of years of life on Earth. Moving through countless strata of time, the soul gathers, collects, and carries forward an immense, incalculable record: a vast, living library containing the entire sum of data antecedent to its new human life. And when the soul is born, it will wear the garments of this rich library like robes woven from a great genetic story now coded in muscle and sinew and fascia, weaving through its veins and nerves and neural networks, in its marrow and memory and emotion.

The soul itself is pure energy, and energy needs a channel, a container. The gametes of two living humans—the parents—offer instructions for the soul to use during its development into form. That form, of course, is the physical body, which will become the soul's vessel throughout its incarnation.

People today often remark on the labor and delivery process as though it were inherently medical or somehow disordered, even referring to one's "repressed birth trauma" and ruminating on its link to present-day suffering. But we might also regard the birth process as a kind of initiation, a rite of passage that bonds the energy of a soul with its human vessel. So, while it is true that a medically difficult delivery may be linked to certain physical, emotional, or psychological effects—and in some cases to impairments in parent-child attachment and bonding[1]—the birth process itself is physically and spiritually natural, a liminal *crossing into* for the newly incarnating soul.

What happens when the soul arrives is just as important as the genetic structure it inherits. When the mother, father, or primary caregiver touches, holds, caresses, and gazes into the eyes of the newborn child, the energy of its soul is invited further into the body. Initially, the soul of the child is pure energy; the parents are the structure, or cup, through which the child's energy emerges and takes shape. When this process is allowed to happen in a healthy way, a safe and grounding *relational* container is made between parents and child, and this, too, forms a structural vessel or cup. After about three months, the subtle veils begin to close so that the energy of the soul can become more fully anchored with the frequency and form of its physical life system. Nature and nurture are interpenetrating influences.

> *The soul itself is an impulse—an arrow of energy, of desire and will.*

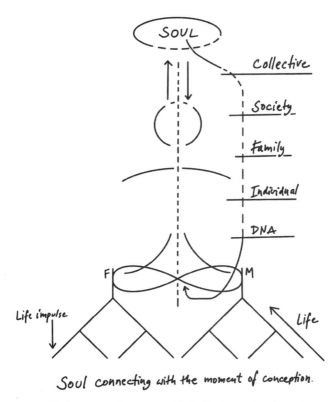

Soul connecting with the moment of conception.

The human soul connects with the body, moving through
systemic layers of the karmic/family grid.

The soul itself is an impulse—an arrow of energy, of desire and will. And for hundreds of thousands of years, human will has expressed a desire for belonging: the fertilized egg "attaches" to and is embraced within the larger vessel of the uterus, thus achieving belonging. If all goes well, the fully developed fetus prepares to leave the uterus, and in the next phase, a tiny human life is delivered into the arms of its mother. Again, it finds belonging. But all souls possess another impulse, which is to stretch, explore, and grow in order to satisfy a curiosity for discovery. These twin desires of the will—for belonging as well as free-dom, for communion as well as autonomy—create a choreographed adagio in figure-eights.

THE INDIVIDUATION LOOP

The infant's urge to crawl begins as an impulse of curiosity, an expression of will. Following this instinct, the baby first gathers herself on four limbs and rocks back and forth. Soon she is propelling her body forward, again and again. With each attempt to crawl, the baby's developing brain and nervous system are wiring the code for "crawling" into the structure of the brain and body. The neural framework for this new behavior descends throughout the body like the roots of a tree, embedding itself into form. As this structure becomes clearer and more concrete, more *space*—more "room" if you will—is created in the body-mind. At the same time, the child begins inhabiting more space in the external world. She crawls a short distance from her mother and stops to look back. She learns in this way about space—the distance between—and also about time: *How long does it take me to get back to Mother? How quickly can I crawl away?* The activity of crawling takes shape in a kind of rhythm: there is desire, movement, space, and repetition until crawling has become a learned competence. Once established, an opening appears for a new impulse and, therefore, new capacities, to flourish. Soon, the baby is standing up to walk—and then to run.

With each new competency we develop, more space *is created for new growth, which allows us room to witness our growth, making it a conscious process.*

In this way, the baby (the new soul) is constantly learning about space, time, and rhythm (STR). Every process, every new learning, every new capacity has STR. If the mother is attuned to the baby, she will sense the child's STR process and neither push the baby to learn too quickly nor hold her back when she is ready. STR is at the heart of the developmental process.

Continuing our look through the mystical lens, we can think of the impulse or will of the soul as an energy that gets channeled into structure, becoming the three-dimensional realization of the body. As we learn and grow, new energy or information gets embodied in the form of new competencies. We learn to crawl, run, count, sing, write, lead, and so on—thus creating greater complexity in form. With each new competency we develop, more *space* is created for new growth, which allows us room to witness our growth, making it a conscious process. From there, new potentials become available to us, and the path begins again at a greater stage of complexity. This is the universal journey from impulse into embodiment into witness. The overall movement can be viewed as the looping of energy-into-structure, the essential dance of development. I refer to this dance as the *individuation loop*.

You and I and everyone we know are continuing the steps of this developmental dance, even through adulthood. Each new stage of learning, growth, and witness makes space for new insight and inspiration to enter and for new capacities to be born.

Now, when a child first begins to explore the world, he is following the soul's impulse to satisfy curiosity and freedom. The baby reaches out to touch or taste or look—and comes back. He reaches out a little farther and comes back. Again and again, he reaches out and loops back. Each time, it is his curiosity that moves him outward to explore his environment, and it is the feeling of uncertainty or fear that draws him back, toward the safety and reassurance of the parent. Seek, return, seek, return: freedom and belonging. This pattern is an expression of the looping rhythm, energy-into-structure.

When a small child encounters something startling or scary in his environment, he runs back to the parent. Sensing the child's fear, the parent picks him up, caresses him, or otherwise assures the child that all is well—nothing to fear. In the process, the parent is reaffirming a safe container for holding and dissolving the child's fear. In this way, parents and caregivers directly assist their children's brains and nervous systems in the process of emotional co-regulation—and eventually, emotional *self*-regulation.

As adults, we tend to think of fear as universally negative or destructive. Often, fear creates blocks in our subjective experience. This is the consequence of unmet anxiety, trepidation, and distress—fear that has not been received in an adequate container of safety and reassurance. On its own, fear is an important emotional impulse, not just for survival but for relation and connection. If the developing child's fear is consistently met with reassurance and safety, the soul experiences belonging, and the body's neurological and emotional structure can easily grow and flourish. Healthy attachment helps generate interior and exterior coherence—plus something else: more space.

Eventually, the impulse of curiosity propels the growing toddler out farther than before, and this time she doesn't feel afraid. When her father calls her back, she proudly resists: "No!" Again, he calls her back; again, the child says, "No!" By resisting or opposing the will of the parent, a toddler is asserting her own will. She is creating a brand-new internal structure: a feeling of self, of *me*. She is individuating. The child is expressing a new desire for autonomy apart from the enmeshed cocoon of the parent-child relationship, where there is boundless safety but very little freedom. Through a new dance of resistance and opposition, the energy of the soul is beginning to crystalize the first structures of its interior dimension, the inner *I*.

This is only possible once the child has created enough healthy internal structure. Resisting or practicing saying "no" strengthens the structure and helps build autonomy. (In order to jump, we need sturdy ground beneath us.) Agency, anger, and resistance are important aspects of this developmental stage.

To claim his autonomy, a young child eventually insists that he be allowed to brush his own teeth or get himself dressed without help. "No, let me do it!" is the common refrain in the households of toddler-age children. It's important that parents support these ventures into independence. When adults fail to get the switch from protection to autonomy, a child will naturally express anger and demand his space and freedom. After all, the soul must stay true to its own process of becoming. If the child is regularly or harshly punished for such expressions, however, a split in the psyche may result between autonomy needs and attachment needs (i.e., between the will to become and the desire to preserve important bonds and to belong).

A growing child will eventually need more space in the family system (broader territory, if you will), which can be difficult for some parents. The art of parenting is about knowing when support is needed versus when giving space (without disconnection) is needed. The right balance of these supports a child's natural development and nourishes their ability to relate with others.

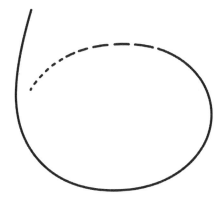

Individuation loop: the process by which energy gets encoded into structure.

VERTICAL AND HORIZONTAL DEVELOPMENT, BELONGING, AND BECOMING

The individuation loop of development emerges through both a vertical axis and a horizontal axis. Imagine a subtle thread being pulled by a needle up and up through the crown of your head. The thread itself is a stream of light, energy, and information that runs along the spine, connecting you vertically down and through your parents' genetic lineages, branching and flowing down and down and down through the roots of countless generations. The roots of this thread continue down into the genetic lineage of our earliest natural ancestors, down through the primates, mammals, vertebrates, and multicelled creatures. The thread roots even further back through the earliest, single-celled life-forms and back down into the body of the earth itself. It reaches all the way back through the planet's earliest constituent salts and minerals, back to the arrival of water, back to carbon, and deeper into the birth and death of stars—to the dawn of the universe itself.

Our children, if we have them, appear ahead of us in that vertical line; they are the fulfillment of an ancient evolutionary desire to become and to belong and to become again anew. In that way, children embody the tip of an evolutionary impulse, which rises from us and seeks out the edge-space of future light, pointing toward our evolutionary potential.

Perpendicular to the vertical axis is the horizontal thread, whose needle moves from us—out and in, out and in—in a process of ever greater enfoldment, weaving our individual lives into the fabric of the communal, societal, global, and cosmic tapestry. When a child first enters school, for example, there is a formation process for developing a new sense of safety and belonging beyond that provided by the family. Once that new container is established, the child can feel herself as part of the school community. Now she experiences belonging at home among family *and* at school. In a wonderful way, her parents form the safety net from which she learns to branch out safely. If she faces difficulty in the school or community, her parents ideally provide protection, comfort, and security so that she can integrate her experiences and bravely venture out again.

Each of us has an inborn desire to belong in the wider world, just as every cell in the body belongs to the body. As a child grows into an adult, he seeks safety and belonging—first with his parents, then with other family and caregivers, then with his school and community, and so on. Belonging is affinity, connection, mutuality, kinship, communion. Wherever we find belonging, we can *become*. We can grow and evolve and express more of our creative, emergent nature. Belonging is a function of horizontal development; becoming is a function of vertical growth. Both unfold naturally as extensions of the healthy individuation loop.

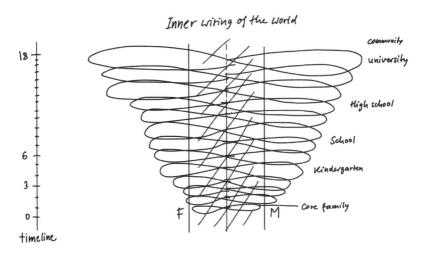

Inner writing of the world

community
university
High school
School
Kindergarten
Core family

18
6
3
0

timeline

F   M

As a child grows, attends school, and joins with community,
ever larger spheres of social belonging are created.

THE NEUROBIOLOGY OF RELATION

When we look at the mystical individuation loop through the lens of contemporary science, we find a startling symmetry. The branches and roots of the central and peripheral nervous systems regulate the body's life functions and allow us to sense, perceive, and respond to the world—and, therefore, to grow. But the nervous system also serves as the central mediator for connection, relation, and belonging. Within it, the vertical and horizontal axes meet.

The body's vagus nerve, the longest and most complex cranial nerve, runs from the brain stem to the colon. This powerful neural highway transmits critical information between the brain and body, mediating vital sensory, motor, and parasympathetic functions so that the heart, lungs, throat, and gut can function.[2] But it does a great deal more. *Vagus* is derived from the Latin for "wanderer," and true to name, this wandering star of the nervous system plays a vital role in social connection.

We all know about the nervous system's primary survival responses, deployed instantaneously when we experience high stress or a life-threatening encounter. These are, of course, the sympathetic fight, flight, or freeze response and the parasympathetic freeze-or-faint response (the freeze response is a combination of sympathetic and para-sympathetic activation).[3] But in 1994, American neuroscientist Stephen Porges, PhD, director of the Kinsey Institute's Trauma Research Center, proposed the *polyvagal theory*, an illuminating model of the nervous system premised on a startling intersection between these elegant and primitive survival responses and human social behavior. Indeed, Porges identified a separate survival response belonging to the nervous system but directly linked to the social environment. He coined this mechanism the *social engagement system* (SES).[4]

Under ordinary conditions, we tend to feel soothed and assured when met with eye contact and a kind smile. We experience pleasure when singing, kissing, and nursing a baby. These and other social behaviors help us feel a sense of safety, security, bonding, and belonging, all of which we need to truly thrive. What is interesting is that our brains and nervous systems become hardwired to detect and decipher even the faintest, nearly imperceptible shifts in our social atmosphere. We learn to read the changing currents in other peoples' facial expressions and micro-expressions; in vocal tone and speech intonation; and in body posture, movement, and more. And we use this social mechanism to almost instantly assess whether our environment is safe and affirming or somehow poses a threat.

As a first-time (or many-time) passenger on an airplane, for example, you might feel a little anxiety. When the plane hits difficult turbulence, that anxiety instantly spikes; now you feel fear. The first thing you will likely do—automatically, without thinking about it—is to look to your neighbors and nearby passengers. Just a quick glance among strangers can convey a feeling of *We're in this together*, and that helps reestablish calm. Shared emotion, an exchanged smile, a mutual laugh of exasperation or relief—any or all of these belong to tend-and-befriend[5] behaviors, expressing the natural instinct of humans to affiliate in times of stress. Affiliation helps us feel calmer, safer, better.

At base, Porges's theory reveals the crucial role that social connection plays in our ability to withstand stress and recover from adversity, even trauma. Indeed, one's ability to reliably interpret the subtle language of the social atmosphere correlates with increased resilience, health, well-being, and positive bonds in relationships. For most, the social engagement system is coded and framed into the nervous system from the moment of our earliest interactions and continues to strengthen as we develop and grow. This, too, is a looping dance of energy-into-structure, or intelligence-into-body. And when this co-regulation process is somehow impeded or stunted, we suffer. We are less able to self-regulate, less able to feel safety or belonging. This can occur as a consequence of early relational wounds, such as we see in developmental or attachment trauma, where the bonds of connection between parent and child are harmed by neglect, abandonment, or abuse (including the inadvertent presence of the parent's own unresolved trauma). When a caregiver is unable to regulate his or her moods, emotions, and energies, the child may experience feelings of terror, anxiety, and uncertainty, with nowhere to turn for reassurance. As a result, the SES cannot establish itself properly in the home *or* the wider world.

When the nervous system does not properly grow and flourish, the energy of the soul does not fully or clearly embody. Instead, it disconnects in some way from the body, dissociates from the emotions, and expresses mental or psychological fragmentation. In this state, the energy of the soul is unable to establish and ground a coherent self-sense or other-sense. When the body, emotions, and mind are dissonant and incoherent, the rhythm of energy-into-substance is out of step. To better understand how and why this happens, we must take a closer look at the phenomenon of trauma.

REAL TIME VERSUS TRAUMA TIME

The instant a traumatic experience happens, we might say that a living snapshot is taken, which captures the sum energy and information of the event, down to the body's subtlest sensations and reactions—and splits that snapshot apart from the lifestream. As the central nervous system laser-focuses on surviving the trauma, this snapshot or fragment gets filed away in the unconscious, to be dealt with at a more advantageous time. In the middle of a life-altering event, there's no time for contemplation (*Ah yes, as this life-threatening thing is happening, I'm feeling this way*), and this is an evolutionary adaptation. All systems are engaged in survival. Nevertheless, a record of living energy has been frozen in time and filed away in the unconscious, buried somewhere in the body.

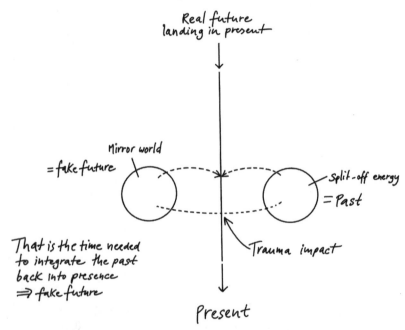

Fragmented energy gets stuck in the past (left side) by splitting the center line, or the present. This creates a false "mirror world"/unreal future (depicted to the right).

Think of it as a bioenergetic record that contains the undigested energy of the trauma. It is a voluble "piece" of the self in spacetime, which becomes frozen or arrested and split away. That is not to say that it *goes* away—it can't. For as long as that trauma aspect remains undigested, a part of the soul's energy remains frozen in time, stuck in shadow, and buried in the body.

Much like dark matter, trauma's shadow is not visible to the naked eye; it can only be observed by its effects on the surrounding system. Suppressed too long, this dark, undigested substance has a way of reemerging in the guise of discomfort, disorder, illness, or disease. The main thing we notice—whether we study the body, the psyche, or the soul—is that unresolved trauma creates dysregulated emotions and out-of-balance responses to one's immediate environment and the people in it. We refer to these as *post-traumatic symptoms*, and they manifest at the extremes of a continuum.

On one end, we see *hyper*arousal: the elevation of the fight, flight, or freeze response. A person in this state may experience increased anxiety, irritability, and/or aggression, or a tendency for hypervigilance (e.g., perpetually scanning the environment for potential danger). Here, the nervous system's innate sympathetic response to stress or danger appears to have been hacked or hijacked, so that it is always "on."

On the other end of this spectrum, we see *hypo*arousal. Here, the nervous system's parasympathetic shut-down response gets hacked, and in the aftermath of trauma, a person may simply shut down, dissociate, or appear numb. This person may express apathy and detachment and may potentially suffer from depression. Of course, the same individual can express both hyper- and hypoarousal symptoms at different times or in different areas of life. Trauma is like a crazy scene in a movie that's suddenly been put on mute. The drama is still going, but there's no sound. Then someone grabs the television and throws it in the ocean. Slowly it sinks into darkness (the unconscious), where the same scene replays without end.

Like any continuum, the extremes alone are not the whole picture. Unforeseen circumstances or signals in the environment may suddenly activate, or "trigger," either set of responses in the same traumatized person—and again, in different ways, at different times. For anyone dealing with unresolved trauma, the dysregulation of the nervous system and emotions can make it difficult to maintain healthy relationships, even with oneself. This is perhaps the greatest consequence of trauma: its impact on one's ability to connect and relate, to feel safety and belonging and togetherness—and, therefore, to grow.

Yet, post-traumatic activations can be looked at another way. When a person becomes suddenly triggered in response to the environment, the original energetic snapshot of undigested trauma may resurface, not simply because there's an injury but as an opportunity to fulfill yet another evolutionary function of the nervous system: to reincorporate undigested energy back into the living system. This is the self-healing function of *integration*.

When we bring consciousness to bear on this process (witness), we discover still higher evolutionary capacities that aid repair. In particular, we awaken the soul's innate ability to help heal others.

THE RESTORATION OF AFTERTIME

If you had a disagreement with your partner over breakfast, you will feel less present in your work until you've had an opportunity to sit and digest the experience. On your drive to the office and throughout the day, you will likely replay moments from the morning's conflict in your mind. You may feel distracted, disconnected, or even anxious. You're still carrying undigested information from the morning, as if your server were too overloaded to process it in time, as it happened. I refer to this state as *aftertime*. In aftertime, it's as if the contents of the morning's conflict are bags of luggage you must drag with you everywhere you go until you can sort their contents. If half of you is consumed with those bags, you can't be fully present—you are half in the past.

Unintegrated history is past; integrated history is presence.

But this is about much more than simple disagreements over toast and coffee. Any one person may be delayed substantially in aftertime and is, therefore, incapable of full presence due to personal traumas that have not been resolved. In the same way, communities and societies that carry significant unresolved cultural wounds are likewise fractured in aftertime, keeping us busy for generations. Aftertime is past energy that has not been fully lived or digested and continues to impede presence today. So, the inverse of aftertime is presence. Unintegrated history is past; integrated history is presence.

Each human soul is an expression of energy moving along a path of vertical and horizontal development. Yet, every human soul is born into interpenetrating fields of ancestral and collective trauma. The human matrix, or collective field, contains so much instability, dissonance, and alienation that we have all in some way been imprinted by these tensions. This, too, is aftertime. And perhaps the greatest consequence of this disequilibrium is the persistent phenomenon of separation.

In aftertime, not only do we feel separate from one another, we feel estranged from our own souls and from our source. Moreover, we feel divided in time: part of us is absorbed in the repetitional past, while another part obsesses over an artificial future. Yet, it is only in the fullness of presence that are we liberated. In presence, we feel greater attunement with the body. We experience a sense of flow, of lightness. We become clearer, more awake, more connected. With presence, there is more space, more movement, more illumination. With presence, we restore the past and realign ourselves in space and time.

When someone you know becomes triggered by past trauma, you can learn to feel into the intelligence of their nervous system with your own. In essence, you can consciously employ the social engagement system to help you both observe and connect with another's pain—and perhaps even assist in its healing.

When a friend, coworker, or therapeutic client becomes suddenly and inappropriately fearful, hostile, withdrawn, or suppressed, you can quietly lean in and notice: *Ah, a hurting four-year-old child is suddenly present in their energy.* Some psychologists refer to this as regression, but the presence of this four-year-old child is pointing to the place in time at which an original trauma occurred. The frightening, undigested experience of the four-year-old has been held apart in a separate "time zone" from the active self. And like a futuristic time traveler, you can locate it. As you do, you begin to notice that this four-year-old aspect has stepped forward so that some of the undigested pain it once experienced may be witnessed and met with safety and reassurance.

In fact, what we think of as destiny is, in truth, the unassimilated past. Trauma never stays buried. Whatever has been left unresolved will recapitulate. It was philosopher George Santayana who first said, "Those who cannot remember the past are condemned to repeat it."[6] Those who cannot fully digest and integrate the past will re-experience it, again and again. Until the shards of trauma have been restored to wholeness, the past just recycles. The Eastern mystical traditions refer to this process as *karma*, from the Sanskrit for "effect" or "fate." Yet, by bridging contemporary scientific understanding with ancient wisdom, we see that karma is the residual energy of unprocessed suffering.

What's more, the existence of unhealed trauma has the power to injure our experience of self and other and to distort our perception of space and time. Like a freeze-frame, trauma's presence glitches and warps the screen of reality so that the emotions, perceptions, and beliefs that we project onto that screen become dysregulated and disrupted. Without integration—the incorporation of past fragments of the self into the whole—the shadows and shades of the past lumber everywhere around us, blocking light and disfiguring our experience of the present.

Whether or not we have experienced trauma personally, we are each born into a field darkened by the consequences of ancestral, cultural, and historical suffering. The mass volatility (hyperarousal) and disaffection (hypoarousal) that we see in contemporary society are the symptoms of the unintegrated past—not in the abstract but in the actual. These extant forces fracture our perspectives and distort our perceptions of self, other, and the world because they hinder our capacities to relate and connect, to synchronize in time and space, and to cohere with one another in the fullness of presence. Many of the consequences of unresolved trauma are taken as "normal"—*That's just how society is; that's just how people are; that's life*—when they are anything but normal.

The good news is that healing ourselves and restoring our communities is possible—and may be far simpler and more powerful than we have come to expect. In the next chapter, we will investigate the practice of presence; the capacity of attunement; and the subtle, energetic competence of synchronizing ourselves in time and space. When strengthened, these practices create a stable foundation for true healing to occur across the personal, ancestral, and communal realms we share.

PRACTICE: STRESS ASSESSMENT AND REDUCTION

Given these turbulent times, attunement practices can help you witness and digest symptoms of stress. The goal of this practice is to help you ground and come into a deeper sense of inner balance so that you can be more present with your external experience. Without inner balance, external experiences are more likely to overwhelm you. You might wish to make a voice recording of the attunement practice being spoken aloud; it can be played anytime you choose to practice. (You can also listen to recordings of Thomas guiding the meditation practices at attunedbook.com.)

First, take a moment to bring your attention into your body. With a couple of breaths, connect with the sensations that feel most vivid right now. Perhaps the chair feels firm beneath you, your hands feel chilled, or your belly is full.

Now turn your attention to any stress you may be feeling in the body. Are your shoulders a bit tense? Is there a feeling of unease or discomfort in your abdomen or chest? Does the mind feel restless or overactive? Scan each area of the body, including the solar plexus, chest, throat, and neck, and simply take notice of the body's current stress level. Is it high, medium, or very low?

Now focus again on your breath. Simply breathe into and out of any areas of stress you noticed, allowing those places in the body to soften with each breath. As you breathe this way, your nervous system will slowly begin to regulate, allowing the body to digest and integrate the stress it is holding.

If you feel overwhelmed by the stress level in your body as you practice, reach out to someone you trust who can support you with co-regulation.

3

The Art of Attunement

Attunement can be simply defined as the focus of attention on the inner world. Interpersonal attunement is the focusing of kind attention on the internal subjective experience of another.
—DR. DAN SIEGEL

If the doors of perception were cleansed, everything would appear to man as it is, infinite.
—WILLIAM BLAKE

An essential proposition of transparent communication is that every human being is composed of a vast living library filled with all possible information; nothing is left out. The ancestral wisdom of our most primordial ancestors resides in our DNA and in every cell of our bodies, brains, and nervous systems. This living library is intricately patterned on all that has been learned by life over countless millennia—much in the way your web browser contains records of all of the websites you visited today and every other day since the last time you cleared its history. If you wanted to know everything you could about how you have spent your life or what people and events have impacted you and how, you need only take a look at your inner library.

Nothing gets deleted; everything is stored right inside you. The moment you were conceived, the day you were born, your first time crawling or walking, your first and last kiss—everything you have ever learned, felt, or experienced is all safely filed away.

This library contains many levels and tiers, each of which stores the knowledge and wisdom you acquired at every stage of your physical and psychological development, plus all that has been passed down to you from your ancestors. When you are in relation with a highly attuned person—someone who is attentive, available, curious, and aware—they can "check out" and review many of the "files" that are housed within you. Are you intellectual? Are you highly social? In what ways are you intuitive? Did you experience a childhood trauma at age three? Or perhaps at age ten when your parents divorced? All of this is readable at the subtle level and is accessible within your subtle body or energy library.

Attunement, like listening, is essential to authentic relating. By practicing attunement with others, you grow in relational wisdom— the facility to see others more clearly, to feel (and feel *with*) them more deeply, and to connect in altogether richer, more authentic ways.

To extend the library metaphor, imagine books on a shelf. If you went looking for a certain book but decided to jog past all the shelves, you'd have a hard time reading any of the titles. In order to select the right book, you need to slow down and *tune in* to absorb the information before you. The same applies when attempting to connect with another person. Mature relationality requires you to slow down and tune in. It's about learning to adjust your "speed" to the other person's so you can better meet and connect. It's about developing the capacity to align your frequency to their frequency, your perception to their perception, your biofield to their biofield.

Every person we meet is a particular movement or arrangement of energy, like a piece of music. Only through deep listening—by attuning and receiving—can we adjust the speed of our movement in order to meet and receive the other deeply and well.

CONNECTING THROUGH ATTUNEMENT

Not long ago, I sat with a one-year-old child who, only a few days before, had been in an accident and was still somewhat in a state of shock. The baby's mother was naturally very concerned. As I sat and played with the child, I tuned in, adjusting my energy to meet his energy, something that requires no words. I consciously slowed my own movement to meet his, so that we could *be* together in a space of relation.

The moment our energies synchronized was quite clear: there was now subtle electricity flowing between us, as if we had created a shared nervous system. I could now perceive patterns of energetic tension in the child's field, created by the shock of his accident. There was a precise sensation of contraction around pain and fear, as though the child had drawn his energy tightly into his body—a survival response—and simply hadn't released that tightness yet, despite no longer being in danger.

By being grounded in my own body, I could offer the child my presence and attunement, and then I was able to adjust my vibration to precisely match his. This allowed my nervous system to extend a little of its acquired resilience to the child's more vulnerable, still-developing nervous system. I simply felt *with* him, conveying an energy of relaxation into the space between us. This had the effect of helping him process some of the fear he was holding, allowing it to shift and release so that he could slowly relax. After only about ten minutes, he became more alert and curious, more actively engaged. Again, no lengthy discussions about the accident or how it had felt or what it all could mean were necessary. Simple presence, attunement, and subtle alignment allowed the innate co-regulatory mechanism to do its work.

PRACTICE: INNER-BODY ATTUNEMENT

This practice is an invitation to go inside and explore the body using inner awareness so you can develop higher attunement abilities. This inner journeying will bring you into deeper relation with the body through inner-body awareness. It is a way of creating or enhancing your inner x-ray vision so that the whole body becomes accessible as a living field of information.

Sit comfortably and bring your focus to the movement of your breath.

As you exhale, relax. Enjoy the simplicity of your body sitting in the chair, on the cushion, or on the floor. Notice your posture. Bring your attention to any sensations of weight or pressure.

Simply rest in the beauty of sitting.

As you drop in, focus on any physical sensations. Notice how the body offers more information, more detail. The attention becomes more refined. There is a higher resolution.

Notice any tension that is present. Feel the sensation (or lack of sensation) that is present in your legs, your hips, your belly, your shoulders, your arms, your head. You are creating an inner body map.

Which areas feel more present and available? Which parts feel darker or more disconnected and absent? Some areas of the body may feel alive with movement and sensation; others may be harder to feel or sense. You may need to concentrate harder on the darker territories.

It's good to simply become aware, to witness without judgment. There is nothing that needs to be changed.

Simply practice increasing the body's resolution by refining your awareness.

If it's hard to connect to the body, respect that. There's no need to create pressure on yourself. Just notice.

Now, tune in more specifically. Notice that your body has bones. What does a bone feel like? Select a bone—perhaps a femur—then tune in and listen. Simply receive the bone's transmission. What is its quality? What visual or other sensory data do you notice as you focus on the femur?

Be playful with any subtle information you receive.

Shift your focus now to a muscle—perhaps one of the quadriceps or hamstrings in your thighs. How relaxed or tense does the muscle feel? How alive or disconnected? As you continue focusing on the muscle, do you notice an inner image, impression, or physical sensation?

Now move your awareness to an organ, such as your liver or heart. See if you can connect with this organ in the same way. As you focus on that area of the body, do you experience an inner image? A sensation? A feeling of more or less energy or aliveness? Is there a sense of relaxation or contraction?

See if you can notice how the organ is communicating with its environment. Is there a feeling of isolation or connection? Notice any intuitive impressions: does the organ seem stressed or free-flowing?

We have all heard the axiom that two heads are better than one. It speaks to the higher intelligence of attunement, a cornerstone of relational wisdom. Whether you notice or not, each time you meet eyes with someone—a stranger, a coworker, a dear friend—a full-body transmission of energy/information is exchanged.

The body-mind is the system with which I relate to others and to my world; it is my instrument. By developing the subtle capacities of my instrument, I learn to tune in—to hear, feel, sense, and see—to any unresolved energies in myself or others, such as the shock and fear felt by the child. I could track the location of these energies in his body by tuning in to my own body and reading the information it conveys. This is all done gently, subtly, quietly. Yet, for the other person, it creates a powerful feeling of being seen, or what Dr. Daniel Siegel, clinical professor of psychiatry at UCLA School of Medicine and founder of the field of interpersonal neurobiology, describes as "feeling felt."[1] It is intrinsic to the nature of children (and all people) that feeling felt is experienced as positive feedback. Feeling felt is a function of relational safety and belonging, and it allows a growing child to open and express even more of who they are. Put simply, feeling seen encourages the human will or soul to continue to flower.

DEVELOPING RELATIONAL ATTUNEMENT

We transmit our inner state directly into our environment. A person in a relaxed, grounded state transmits a relaxed, grounded energy into their environment. This is something other people can feel. When we enter that space, our nervous systems directly receive the transmission, and most of the time it has a relaxing, grounding effect on us, like a warm blanket of belonging. Of course, we can be so busy with ourselves that we are not aware of the transmission, but if we are present and attuned, the exchange is obvious. (It is quite a beautiful feeling to meet and interact with people who *are* present.)

The more embodied and available you are, the more clearly you see the world. Heightened perception is a function of presence, and it has an innate developmental potential. Many successful businesspeople are successful because they are highly attuned to the movements of their businesses. As a result, they are frequently able to sense what is coming, sometimes three steps ahead. Presence functions similarly in the relational space. When you are present, available, and attuned to others, your sense perceptions are heightened and clarified; you become more intuitive.

When we practice transparent communication, we are listening deeply to the other with our whole bodies, allowing us to perceive even the subtlest cues, impulses, and threads that may appear. The word *transparent* refers to these subtle threads and layers of energy and information that are accessible through the intersubjective and transpersonal dimensions, the subtle space between us.

Imagine two people—let's call them Peter and Adele. Together, they head to a café, order their coffees, and sit down across from one another to talk. Perhaps they spend an hour this way, sitting and chatting over steaming cups. Eventually, Adele begins sharing a difficult story about her past. If Peter is attuned and listening deeply, he will notice the slightest instances in which it feels as though Adele has disappeared from the space, even as she's talking. It is as if by mentioning some aspect of her past she simply vanishes, just for a second, leaving her body and the present moment. Perhaps there is a second that her eyes appear to zoom very far out, as though she is no longer seeing Peter but something in the distance, accompanied by a feeling of hollowness behind her voice. Peter can still hear Adele talking, but it's as if the line drops and she is no longer available.

These sorts of disconnections happen all the time in the course of ordinary relating. One person's energy may suddenly contract, perhaps unconsciously as an avoidant or dissociative response. These instances are symptoms formed by an originating disconnection, an earlier place of injury, isolation, or trauma—a bit like encountering a small scratch on a record or a snag in the loop.

If Peter is unaware of these subtle cues, he may be very surprised after six months or a year of dating to learn that Adele experienced a past trauma or that it is still occupying a significant portion of the energy she might otherwise have available for their relationship.

Very often it is the unconscious recognition of one another's wounds that brings two people together in a romantic relationship. The unresolved pain belonging to one partner is like a key that perfectly fits the lock made by the unresolved pain in the other. Often, a pair like this feels an intense, even overwhelming, connection and quickly becomes romantically involved without recognizing their traumatic bond. After six months or a year, when the relationship becomes problematic and painful, both parties are often taken totally by surprise. How was it that they could fall so madly in love only to have it sour so quickly? (We could think of marriage as a process of learning and becoming aware of everything we missed about our spouse when we first fell in love.)

Many times, a client will sit down and immediately begin sharing an emotionally charged story about his or her relationship dynamic. "Listen, Thomas, I had an argument with my wife," a man might say, "and this is what happened." He then launches into the dramatic details as he sees them, usually a recapitulation of who was "right" and who was "wrong." If I'm not fully present and attuned, I could be hypnotized by his story, finding that I agree or disagree with the reported behaviors of his wife. But if I listen from a deeper place, with my whole body, I may notice that, as my client is describing the details of his relationship crisis, his energy is no longer present in his legs and feet—as if he's no longer standing on the ground. There is an energetic absence in his lower body, and he has lost touch with physical sensation there. Tuning in more, I sense that he is contracted in his upper torso or head, or that he is absorbed by and responding from fear, as if in a survival defense posture. It is the energy of fear, then, that the man is avoiding or *absencing*, perhaps so that he can feel strong rather than vulnerable. And if he has less life force anywhere in his body, his awareness is diminished there. That part of him will be invisible to him. Simply put, the man has interpreted his relationship saga as so threatening that he can no longer stay grounded enough to process it.

When the energy center at the base of your spinal column is weak, you are ungrounded. There is no connection to the earth beneath your feet, and you might come across to others as restless, detached, adrift, or disconnected. Falling is the most primal biological fear instinct; all healthy infants experience it. We contract our energy and remove it from the base in reaction to a fear (often unacknowledged and unprocessed) about a threat to our survival. It is vital that we become aware of when we "leave the ground" as this is a signal from the body that there is something that needs our attention. To continue forward as mature, healthy adults, we need to explore this fear. Whether it appears in ourselves or in others, simply staying present and attuned to it rather than making it "wrong" is a compassionate act, one that allows us to gently restore embodied relation.

CREATING INNER AND OUTER COHERENCE

The verb *cohere* refers to the creation of a unified whole; integration is, therefore, an act of coherence. We are each a dynamic interplay between the physical, emotional, and mental aspects of the self. When we express internal coherence, or synchronization, across all three aspects, we become more present and can more clearly sense, perceive, and attune with our environment. When practicing transparent communication, we are focused on understanding the degree of alignment and flow between the body, mind, and emotions—our own and other people's—and observing how these centers of awareness connect with our external environment.

Can you think of a time you were talking to someone and noticed that their words seemed to contradict their body language? People often say one thing but feel another. With contemplative practice, areas of seeming contradiction become clearer and more evident. Your task, of course, is simply to note the energy without judgment. Transparent communication allows us to see when, where, and how internal and external misalignment is surfacing. It is about learning the language of coherence.

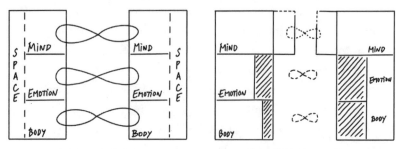

The figure on the left shows two people relating from a high degree of inner coherence between mind, emotions, and body, where space represents inner spaciousness. The figure to the right shows two people attempting to relate from a low degree of inner coherence. As a result, they lack spaciousness and may over-mentalize without feeling or sensing one another in a deeper way.

Practicing higher attunement allows us to establish conscious relational space in which we can better notice and feel any symptoms of incoherence or disconnection. By simply becoming aware of what is present, you can attend to these symptoms with presence and compassion.

Let's say Adele comes to you to talk about a relationship dilemma. As you listen, you might say, "I can feel in my own body how stressful this must be for you right now!" because if you are attuned, you will be able to feel Adele's response to her experience *with* her. When she agrees that her relationship problem is stressing her out, you might gently invite her to stay with the feeling of the stress for a moment, simply allowing it and being present for it.

We never solve these sorts of stresses with our heads alone, after all. However, if we feel back down into our bodies, tracking where the sensation called *stress* is located and noticing what it looks and feels like, we can often learn a great deal that is beneficial—even healing. We might discover, for example, that this thing we have been calling *stress* is actually an unacknowledged, untended sadness or anger that has been hiding out somewhere in the body. Perhaps it has taken the form of an absence and disconnection of energy. Or maybe this fear-energy shows up as an uncomfortable constriction or a painful a knot. As long as the fear goes unwitnessed, Adele will feel too agitated to truly sit with her experience. But if she allows herself to investigate it by simply moving her awareness into the sensation, she may notice whether her fear is a response to a perceived threat or an actual one, new or old. Just by being with the agitation for a while, the energy may shift, relaxing the tension it had been holding and allowing Adele to come back into relation with herself and with others.

This is very important: only when we are grounded and in tune with ourselves can we feel connected and in tune with another person. Using higher attunement, you can connect more fully with yourself and make yourself more available to the other person. Without grounded co-relation (in which both parties are embodied, attuned, and intentional in their interaction), you might find yourself activated or triggered by something in Adele's story when it touches unresolved feelings you have about your own romantic relationship. Or if your fear remains unconscious and unfelt, you might try giving Adele advice that is coming from your fear. However, if you are in true relation with Adele, you will be able to host her within you. With grounded presence, you will begin to notice subtle details that had been invisible to you before.

By consciously choosing to stay open and connected to what you are feeling or sensing, you provide an unspoken but very real support for others who are connecting with you.

Being truly present with another person is among the most precious gifts you can offer. After just a short time together this way, Adele will start to feel a little more grounded and relaxed too. Your grounded, relaxed nervous system has a co-regulatory function for Adele's nervous system. By consciously choosing to stay open and connected to what you are feeling or sensing, you provide an unspoken but very real support for others who are connecting with you.

Our task, then, is to anchor ourselves in the authentic process of listening: to connect with the other person's mental energy, to witness and host his emotional energy, to be present with his physical form. When we are more retracted and energetically closed, the amount of energy and higher intelligence that can flow through us is likewise restricted. We cut off the valve to emergent wisdom, to future flow. Instead of feeling connected with others and open to what is present, we exist in relation to the past. But by consciously practicing grounded attunement, we make ourselves more available to the process of being and becoming. Grounded attunement raises our capacity to respond to our experiences and enhances our resilience. It increases our ability to intelligently respond rather than react. These are all important ways that we accept *response-ability* for our lives, allowing us to live more deeply into the "wake up, grow up, clean up, and show up" directive described by American philosopher and integral theorist Ken Wilber. Really showing up takes commitment and practice.

Of course, we may set out to be grounded, intentional, and embodied as we relate with others, yet find our interactions uncomfortable or even difficult. I'm often asked, "What do I do when I encounter resistance from the other person?" If your intention is to be in a space of healthy relation, then the answer is quite simple: *be with it*. Be with the resistance. Notice it, feel it. After all, if you have set a precondition that the other person must be fully open throughout your exchange, you have already limited the interaction! Any resistance you feel from them will cause *you* to contract, to pull away. You may have shown up to the experience with a *yes*, but when you felt the other's *no*, you quickly expressed a *no* to match it. Meeting resistance with resistance is rarely effective at sustaining connection. Bringing awareness to the process is the point; awareness enhances coherence, which increases space and clarity and opens the door to healing relation.

By creating a daily, ongoing awareness practice, we cultivate mature perspective and the capacity to relate with others, which is an ongoing process—one that requires humility and a willingness to stay open to the new and to accept not knowing.

THE THREE-SYNC PRACTICE

We might think of coherence as an optimum condition, in which the mind is alert, the heart is open and receptive, and the body is energized and balanced. Although this is true, more than anything, coherence is the ability to be present with the experiences of the mind, the heart, and the body—whatever they are—while engaging directly with life. The idea of creating sustained personal coherence may sound a bit aspirational or ambitious to some, but in truth, we can all experience greater coherence with practice.

As you go about your day, simply practice being aware of what is happening inside you while simultaneously being present for whatever is happening outside you. In other words, as you engage with others (your colleagues, your partner, your neighbor) and as you go about your daily routines (responding to email, delivering a presentation, cooking dinner), practice noticing what is arising in your interior landscape. What sensations are present in the body? What thoughts or emotions are here? By regularly witnessing our interiors *as we experience* our exteriors, we can begin to develop a greater sense of alignment and wholeness—what I call *inner/outer coherence*.

I call this process the *Three-Sync Practice*. Again, the aim is simply to make conscious our interiors—our physical, mental, and emotional experiences—as we practice being present to our exteriors (work, relationships, life). As we practice, we deepen self-contact with our vulnerability and an expanded sense of our own humanity.

When the great mystics sat in contemplation, they were, in effect, enhancing the resolution on their perspective, their view of the world. The closer we look at a low-resolution digital photograph, the more pixilation, blur, and lack of clarity we perceive. With increased resolution comes increased coherence, which brings new insights and new clarity into view. When the physical, emotional, and mental bodies are in sync, coherence is heightened. We feel less fragmented, more whole, more integrated. More space is available through which we can access new and higher potential resources.

Remember: this work is an ongoing, dynamic process rather than a series of failure-proof steps or techniques. And the first step of any contemplative process is simply about becoming aware.

PRACTICE: THE THREE-SYNC TECHNIQUE

The Three-Sync Practice is an awareness-based practice to assist you in creating greater inner/outer coherence. You can use it to create greater awareness in and of the body, mind, and emotions—and, therefore, greater coherence between them. The technique can be used regularly or as needed, and it can be modified to best suit your present needs. You might wish to read through the practice fully and then repeat it to yourself in your own words during a quiet meditation. Or, you could make an audio recording of yourself reading the practice aloud, to be played during your practice.

Begin the Three-Sync Practice with a brief check-in. How do you feel in your body? How well are you able to feel the various parts of your body?

If it's helpful to you, take a couple of deep breaths. As you do, slow down the exhalation, dropping into your bodily perception.

Notice your posture—and the fact that you are breathing. Notice the sensation of sitting. How does it feel in your pelvis?

Now notice, if you can, any finer sensations, such as tingling, streaming, or pulsing sensations—wherever they may be in your body.

As you observe these sensations, you're tuning in with the body's data flow. The nervous system animates your bodily perception. (It's very sophisticated information technology.)

Within your body, you might be able to notice areas that feel denser, tense, or perhaps absent, where it's more difficult to connect to any sensation. Perhaps these are stress patterns being communicated in the flow of data. If you can, simply allow yourself to embrace with compassion whatever sensations you feel in the body.

You might notice a feeling of "flow" or areas of open perception and resourced groundedness. Or you might sense areas of tension, stress, or disconnection. Perhaps you are even hosting these together. Simply notice.

Now, shift your attention to your emotional body. What does your emotional experience feel like to you in this moment? Is there any emotion to be identified? Or is there perhaps a bit of numbness or a feeling of disconnection? Simply notice whatever is present and embrace your experience with compassion.

Check in now with the mind. Is your mind busy, open, tight, curious, relaxed, calm? Simply notice and allow.

Ask yourself: *What is it that's aware of me noticing the activity of my mind? What part of me is awareness itself?*

If what you feel and sense and perceive are the letters of a book, what is the paper? What is the space that gives information and perception a place to exist?

As you notice spacious awareness, consider for a moment all the other people who are reading or will read these pages, all the other people who have practiced or will practice in a similar way. Wherever they are in the world, right now, many thousands of people are tuning in to the breath, to the body, to the mind, to the emotions, to the spaciousness within and around them, and to awareness itself. As you open your awareness

> to those other people, you might be able to sense the presence of a whole community that is here, right now, practicing with you. Indeed, you have the capacity to *sense the wider field* and to perceive information that is stored in the social fabric.
>
> Now, without disconnecting from that wider field, slowly take a breath and release it.

Optimum inner/outer coherence is ultimately expressed as a vital balance between space and structure, space and energy, and space and information. Are you connecting to your own inner guidance? Are you able to hear its whisper and follow its compass needle? Are you learning to sense the subtle layers of information within and around you? When there is insufficient inner/outer coherence, there is too much "noise." Everything is a little too loud, making it difficult to hear inner wisdom or tune in accurately to the subtle dimensions. Cultivating a sense of inner spaciousness or stillness enables us to reduce the noise so that we can more clearly hear the still, small voice of intuition and inner guidance and the whisper of the future.

Of course, inner space and silence are independent of external noise. I frequently hear students complain that they find it too hard to meditate without complete silence. And, in response, I may recommend meditating on the subway, in a busy park, at the office, or at home with all the sounds of family around. As the mystical traditions teach us, true stillness cannot be disturbed; true peace cannot be disrupted. Learning to stay connected to your own stillness amidst the noise of the world is a vital practice for our times.

The mystics practice keeping an open window. Imagine an empty window open on your computer desktop. Nothing fills it: no applications, no files, nothing to work on. The only thing present inside the window is your computer's source code, which is always running silently in the background. As you carry out the routines of daily life—from work to childcare to dinner with friends—you can keep an open window, a space within you that is always in touch with source and available to new wisdom, new light.

Fares Boustanji teaches energetic dynamics to leaders and corporate teams with the help of large, powerful birds of prey, including eagles, falcons, and other raptors. When he first began working with them, Boustanji didn't understand why it was that when he allowed the birds to fly freely, they sometimes returned to him at the sound of his whistle and other times refused. Five years later, he knew the answer.

Cultivating a sense of inner spaciousness or stillness enables us to reduce the noise so that we can more clearly hear the still, small voice of intuition and inner guidance, along with the whisper of the future.

These regal creatures can only be in true relationship with humans when we are fully grounded in our own energy—centered in our bodies rather than distracted by our thoughts and feelings. To be worthy of the respect of a Cooper's hawk or a golden eagle—and, therefore, to receive its trust—one must be fully present and embodied. As Boustanji says, "To get in contact with the other, you have to be in contact with yourself."[2]

By engaging with life as an ongoing practice of awareness and coherence building, we learn to hone the art of attunement as a balance of interior and exterior, self and other, being and belonging.

4

The Art of Transparent
Communication

*The more we let go of the protective constrictions throughout
our body, the more we open to and realize ourselves as the
disentangled ground of fundamental consciousness.*
—JUDITH BLACKSTONE

*Attention without feeling, I began to learn, is only a report. An
openness—an empathy—was necessary if the attention was to matter.*
—MARY OLIVER

n 1973, biologist Rupert Sheldrake was busy studying plant development at Cambridge and became interested in the concept of
morphogenic—form-shaping—fields. He intuited that such fields
might play a vital role in plant development but recognized they could
not be passed down genetically. This obstacle triggered a profound
insight, the deeper investigation of which became his hypothesis for
morphic resonance, which Sheldrake would later propose as an underlying organizational pattern for life. "In self-organizing systems at all
levels of complexity," he writes, "there is a wholeness that depends on a
characteristic organizing field of that system, its morphic field."[1] Some
forty years later, Sheldrake explained:

> Morphic resonance is the influence of previous structures of activity on subsequent similar structures of activity organized by morphic fields. It enables memories to pass across both space and time from the past. . . . What this means is that all self-organizing systems, such as molecules, crystals, cells, plants, animals, and animal societies, have a collective memory on which each individual draws and to which it contributes. In its most general sense, this hypothesis implies that the so-called laws of nature are more like habits.[2]

I teach and write about the same concepts—"collective memory," living structures, and human habit—in a not dissimilar way: we are all born into and shaped by various collective fields, a macro representation of what our own bodies and psyches express individually. These nested fields or matrices contain and carry our social memory, social architecture, and habits—from universal human archetypes to specific languages and cultural codes. All people and all societies shape and are shaped by them; they are morphogenic.

Presencing pioneers Peter Senge, Otto Scharmer, and their colleagues elaborate on Sheldrake's concept of morphic resonance this way:

> Every cell contains identical DNA information for the larger organism, yet cells also differentiate as they mature—into eye, heart, or kidney cells, for example. This happens because cells develop a kind of social identity according to their immediate context and what is needed for the health of the larger organism. When a cell's morphic field deteriorates, its awareness of the larger whole deteriorates. A cell that loses its social identity reverts to blind, undifferentiated cell division, which can ultimately threaten the life of the larger organism. It is what we know as cancer.[3]

At the collective scale, shadow, trauma, and the fragmentation they create within humans and among human societies do much the same. (We will examine these concepts in further detail in chapter 6.)

Just as refining the art of attunement is crucial to authentic relating—to transparent communication—a deeper understanding of what we are as individuals and how we function as a community of beings is vital.

DEVELOPING AWARENESS OF INNER-BODY COMMUNICATION

As children, we all learned about the five gross senses, each associated with its own physical sense organ: eyes, ears, tongue, nose, and skin. Later, we may have learned about additional senses, such as balance, proprioception (the sense of movement and position in space), and interoception (the sense of the internal body, such as when you feel thirsty, hungry, cold, or hot). In addition to these bodily perceptions, we possess many subtle senses, including cognition, emotion, intuition, resonance or dissonance, and other impressions, any of which may arise independently or in combination with physical sensations and mental or emotional impressions. Most of us pay far less attention to the finer, subtler information we receive, yet it often holds essential information—a truth that our world's many spiritual traditions have been pointing to for millennia.

As we discussed in the previous chapter, by utilizing a practice of attunement, we become better able to perceive our internal and external worlds together and in higher resolution. And however high the resolution we achieve, a still higher level is always possible. The mystics say that we live simultaneously in a physical universe and a subtle universe (information field). Our physical bodies create the central locus of our awareness in the third dimension, but we also exist as empty space. We are at once particle and wave.

We've all experienced the limitations of the physical universe; we have fallen off bicycles or run into solid objects while walking through a crowd of people (or in our own living rooms!). We all know the pain of failing to pay close enough attention as we jog through a park or walk at nighttime in bare feet. With transparent communication, we learn to look out for the sensation of energetic resistance and energetic obstacles that we encounter in the relational dimension.

For example, you learn to perceive more clearly what a *no* feels like coming from another person, even when they haven't yet spoken the word. You learn to feel this sensation of resistance (defense pattern), like bumping into a closed door. If you're unaware of this subtle resistance, you will miss its cues and may push too far, which creates a feeling of pressure in the other person—a pressure that will be relayed back so that both of you are made uncomfortable as a result. The resistance and discomfort you feel will actually begin to lower the available life force inside you. You might experience this as a feeling of tension and then attempt to compensate for it or suppress it. Whether consciously or unconsciously, you will feel that something isn't right.

Perhaps later, as you walk away, you'll feel tremendous relief that the conversation is over, but the fact that resistance, tension, and discomfort were present are signals that you spent that time with the other person in an unconscious space. You missed something, and that has consequences: you may feel tired or confused or even a little disturbed or irritated after the fact. Maybe you start talking about the other person to a friend to try to get clearer about what happened, an attempt to resolve the unprocessed energy between you.

Karma is postponed experience.

If you walk away from a situation, meeting, or conversation with a lower degree of vitality or aliveness than you had when you arrived, you know you've missed something. Our life energy is an important indicator or gauge for conscious processes.

The Eastern traditions referred to this unprocessed residue as karma: untended energy from the past that continues to surface in one's present. In other words, karma is postponed experience. The presence of karma creates an irritation, which is a signpost about the shadow: each time I experience irritability, a notification bell is ringing in my awareness. If I let myself notice the sensation and feel what it's asking of me, the disturbance can be transformed into a blessing.

When understood this way, we see that feeling and noticing the irritation itself is a subtle perception. And there are many others: moments of resistance, exhaustion, and depletion, for example. These sensations need not be felt as negative, but rather as subtle indicators pointing to an opportunity to look deeper, to create more inner awareness, more inner space, and more attunement and availability to what exists. This process is about both listening and perceiving, which means that it is a kind of inner communication.

RELATIONAL MYSTICISM

In transparent communication, there are two facets to listening. The first requires that you make space within you to receive, not just to respond. As you listen attentively to a colleague, friend, partner, or acquaintance, you can lend part of your attention to the condition of your inner space and what's happening there. How open and relaxed do you feel as you listen? Do you have room inside you to welcome their words and feelings? How much space do you have available for receiving their communication? What sensations show up inside you as you communicate? It is about taking in the other person's words and allowing yourself to be touched by what has been shared.

Let's say that you find yourself in disagreement with someone, perhaps even very strong disagreement. Does your sense of inner spaciousness shrink or contract? Do you feel yourself internally pushing back against or even blocking their words and intentions? Do you feel yourself becoming harder? More rigid? What emotions do you feel coming from the other person? In difficult conversations there is often a closing down or separation that occurs. When that happens, the rest of the discussion can become like a ping-pong match: words are volleyed across a net, but feelings, ideas, and other perceptions are no longer shared and received.

True listening requires open space and brings a quality of relaxation and openness forward. The deepest listener is awake consciousness—in other words, the deepest place in you that listens is pure awareness. This style of listening is a receptive and, therefore, feminine capacity. It allows you to take in and be touched by others' ideas, viewpoints, feelings, motivations, intentions, and life circumstances. At its root, deep listening is about receiving life with an open heart. Strengthening this capacity allows you to be more available to life and to respond from your authentic core. The ability to listen in this way unfolds as you open to greater stillness, presence, and emptiness.

The second facet of listening in transparent communication pertains to attunement. If you and I are sitting together in a noisy, crowded restaurant, it will likely be difficult to hear each other. If I start talking about something important to me, you may struggle to follow. If it's important that you hear me, you will probably lean in and concentrate keenly on my mouth and the sound of my voice. In her book *Gathering Moss*, Robin Wall Kimmerer, a botanist and member of the Bear Clan of the Potawatomi, writes: "Straining to hear a faraway voice or catch a nuance in the quiet subtext of a conversation requires attentiveness, a filtering of all the noise, to catch the music."[4] You will focus as much of your awareness as possible on me, to the exclusion of the clamor and distraction around us. I will need to be precise with my words so that you can follow, and when you speak, I will likewise strive to anchor my awareness in you.

When something is important to us, we find the ability to give it our single-minded focus. This capacity is sought after and strengthened in the spiritual traditions, where one sign of a highly refined meditative practice is the capacity for clear, laser-focused attention. When you achieve this state, your awareness becomes pointed: clear, precise, and specific. Thus, while stillness, presence, and emptiness are universal in nature, attunement is highly specific. Attunement is about precision and particularity.

In this way, sustained contemplative practice guides the practitioner toward higher realization of both the vast and deeply universal and toward a refined perception for the clear and pointedly specific. As you sit in the stillness of deep meditation, there is only the silence of pure awareness. You can rest for hours in this state: no body arising, no emotion arising, no thought arising—only the great magnetic presence of expanded awareness. As you continue to deepen your practice, you discover a higher capacity for hosting the world and your life within. You can hold all of it in your awareness in both its specificity and its vastness. This, in turn, increases your ability to attune to and make space for everything you encounter.

This describes a deeply participatory practice I call *relational mysticism*. Instead of seeking realization in seclusion or by retreating from ordinary life, we create a living practice that remains constant even while we engage with the quotidian demands of work, family, community, and culture. It is a spiritual practice of embodiment across the personal and transpersonal domains. We awaken within the context of the world and the contemporary marketplace, not apart from them. It is, therefore, a deeply immersive, co-creative, procultural impulse in which we are led by our love of humanity and our belongingness to it to care for one another and for the world—both its beautiful and its difficult parts. As cultural mystics, we study the book of life.

Relational mysticism is a deep commitment we make to life. We are alive, which means we are here when it feels great to be here, and we are here when it feels really hard, too. We commit ourselves to all of it, to something bigger than the avoidance of pain and the search for pleasure. We commit ourselves deeply to our daily responsibilities, including our partners, our children, and our work. We commit ourselves to the contributions we're led to make: we commit to our community, to our society, to our planet. We commit to the paradox of nonduality, of *not oneness*, which is that we are all one and yet we are each utterly specific, wholly unique. These truths exist in fluid, dynamic unity, and we are each called forth as participant and as witness.

STUDYING THE BOOK OF LIFE

As we have seen, every human being is a vast library of information, including energy, data, and intelligence, and we are each finely adapted receivers. It is a higher human capacity, as much as it is a birthright, to be able to dial in to one another across multiple channels and modulations. With refined awareness of the subtle signals we transmit, including information about our past, present, and future, we can listen, perceive, and communicate across multiple frequencies and dimensions.

If you want to listen to music while driving, you turn on the radio and look for a station that's playing something good. As you scan through the channels, you're hit with the sounds of all kinds of music, news, "talk radio" programming, and likely some static. Some channels come in clearly, while others are weak and difficult to hear. Then you find your song.

At its heart, transparent communication emanates from the principle of *interabiding unity*, a term attributed to Cynthia Bourgeault.[5] I listen, I take you in, I attune. I receive you within me. I hear your intelligence. I feel your shadows. I sense your beauty. I perceive something of your past, your present, and your future. I hear your song, which is like mine and yet is wholly unique in all the universe.

Every human being transmits and receives all manner of music, including past, present, and future chords. Together, we enact living research on a path to discover the power of transmission and reception (or perception) and to practice attuning to new channels, higher frequencies, and deeper amplitudes. Transparent communication invites us toward a recognition that life holds all the information we may possibly need and that our job is learning how to receive it and how to read the book of life.

Every moment, every situation in which you find yourself, contains the whole book, all the information you may ever need. Whether you are taking a walk, sitting in your workspace, visiting with friends, spending time with your loved ones, or meditating alone, you are able, continually, to study life and to deepen your understanding.

TRANSPARENT COMMUNICATION IS AN EVOLUTIONARY PRACTICE

In *Dogs That Know,* Sheldrake writes:

> Morphic fields hold together and coordinate the parts of a system in space and time and contain a memory from previous similar systems. Human social groups such as tribes and families inherit through their morphic fields a kind of collective memory. The habits, beliefs, and customs of the ancestors influence the behavior of the present, both consciously and unconsciously.[6]

Much of what we call instinct, he says, might also be called collective habits. They are the impulses and behaviors refined by evolution over countless generations. While many of our instincts or habits have aided us for centuries, certain habits and structures inevitably become restrictive, obsolete, or insufficient in helping us meet contemporary realities. They, therefore, prevent us from accessing potential futures.

As you sit and talk with a friend or colleague, older structures and habits within you will ping against older structures and habits in them, and you mutually reinforce these older patterns. However, when there's enough space inside you, you're able to witness the pattern as it surfaces instead of becoming identified with it. You notice your habits as objects in consciousness instead of unconsciously experiencing them as subject or self. This combination of space and witness does a profound thing: it allows for something new to emerge—perhaps a new way of thinking about or dealing with our present situation—a new evolutionary potential. New structures in consciousness.

Through the practice of presencing, which you'll learn throughout this book, you can still yourself long enough to notice, sense, and feel all that arises in the present moment. You become more fully aware, more awake. By presencing yourself and your interior consciousness, you open a portal to new light and to higher information and new personal capacities. By presencing *one another*, you and I do the same; we make space for higher light and newfound relational competencies. We discover new ways of connecting. As higher relational capacities enter us, they are simultaneously downloaded and made available as part of the collective human experience. That way, what we learn together becomes a more accessible probability for others.

Communication itself is an evolutionary process—and an endlessly fascinating area of study. Within our bodies, heart cells communicate with other heart cells. Nerve cells communicate with other nerve cells. And all cells communicate with the whole. In the new field of *plant neurobiology*, scientists study how plants communicate and even process and store information. Many such scientists, including American-Israeli plant geneticist Daniel Chamovitz, propose that plants are able to "see, feel, smell—and remember." Similarly, in another realm (that of the very small), physicists tell us that even at a great distance, quantum objects that interact with each other remain permanently correlated or entangled, a process referred to as *quantum nonlocality*, which looks strangely like a form of instant communication.[7]

Human communication is likewise developmental and evolutionary in nature: as we repeat steps or pathways in the process, prior structures of relating get reinforced. But when those structures become limited, we can restructure to bring in the new. We can rewire or rewrite the underlying code. To do this, we must stay consciously open to *emergence*, to that which is coming into being rather than staying fixed in past assumptions, habits, or tendencies. Emergence occurs when we relate in mutual witness to create more space, more presence, and more attunement—even and especially when past relational patterns show up again.

If you and I are talking and you say something that activates or triggers the past within me, I'm likely to contract and become more rigid. You've tapped into something held within my system from the past, and a cascade of downstream effects unfolds, though you and I will notice only the tip of the iceberg, which is my reaction. If I pause to consider what's happening, I may notice a sudden contraction or feeling of tightness in my heart. In that contracted state, I cut myself off from you as much as from my own potential and my future light.

The moment I react, I have no future; I become bound only to physical, mental, and emotional habits belonging to the past. Whatever I say or do comes from prior conditioning rather than from a novel or creative approach to the present. But if my conditioned patterns haven't solved my problems before, they're unlikely to do so now. Re-solving is about finding a new solution. Resolving a relationship conflict is about emerging into newness together. It is about creating emergent relationships.

In an emergent relationship—even in a long-term marriage, for example—there is only our moment-to-moment meeting, our moment-to-moment relating. We participate consciously and continually, forever. By relating from emergence, we find that even someone we have known for many years is always and eternally new; we're never finished discovering each other. Emergent relationships challenge us to be truly response-able to one another and to whatever arises within and between us. We're asked to show up as receptive, mutual witnesses capable of creating more space and more presence. In this way, we co-create a field of love.

Each time you become more aware of and receptive to a previously unconscious aspect of yourself, that fragmented piece of you is invited back into the fold, and you become more whole as a human being.

RELATIONAL FLOURISHING

When we practice transparent communication, we are engaging in a community of practice. The developmental capabilities we access together become available to all.

The first test is always one's own internal change. You have an insight, integrate an aspect of shadow, or have an awakening experience, all of which means that more of your future potential becomes visible and available to you in the present. Each time you become more aware of and receptive to a previously unconscious aspect of yourself, that fragmented piece of you is invited back into the fold, and you become more whole as a human being. This creates a new opening for your life force, and you feel a rise in energy that can then be channeled toward your growth.

Note the similarities between this kind of integration and the ancient shamanic tradition of soul retrieval or the indigenous tradition described by psychotherapist and author Eduardo Duran as the healing of the "soul wound." At its heart, integration work has a relationship to mystery. Perhaps this is why it is possible for even a single, ground-shifting healing—a sudden and irrevocable shift or awakening and integration—to occur. This is the kind of healing that requires no follow-up sessions; it reaches all the way through.

Most of the time, however, we are like a fragile houseplant, struggling to grow in a north-facing window. When there is just enough care, just enough light, we flower. And when we connect with others who share a similar insight or quality of inspiration in their journey, it feels like a kind of fertilizer for our growth; there is a relational flourishing. My future meets *your* future, and they glimmer together inside us, sparking new insights and ideas. When we have an inspiring dialogue, we touch the future, pulling it toward us so that it becomes more possible, more real. If others join in, we create a shared field that stabilizes our insights by creating new structures in consciousness. In this transpersonal dimension, light enters: the cultural energies—our collective habits, patterns, and structures—become less dense so that new impulses and new manifestational powers break free. As a community of practitioners, we generate new templates for humanity's future.

In truth, what we call *transparent communication* is a cover story for engaging with life as social and relational mystics. A social mystic is a deeply spiritual practitioner within the cultural framework or the contemporary marketplace. As social mystics, we've come out of the caves and ashrams, the hermitages and the monasteries, to stand together as a cultural force. Collectively, we inhabit both our belonging and our becoming.

Otherwise, we find ourselves sacrificing one for the other. We may forgo our becoming—our development or personal evolution—out of a fear of losing social belonging. Or we may sacrifice belonging—abstaining from deeper commitments to relationships, to groups, or to our community—out of a fear that these commitments will arrest our becoming. Maybe we have good reason for our fears. In the past, we may have found ourselves in families or social networks in which we couldn't quite breathe; there wasn't enough space for growth *and* belonging.

As a social mystic, however, you engage in a deeply participatory practice of awareness. You allow yourself to notice how your relationships feel to you, including your relationship with your community and society. As you do, bring yourself into presence with what you are noticing and take a higher resolution. This is purification work, and it allows you to attend to your individual growth as much as to your community of practice and connection.

In his book *Cosmos and Psyche*, author and cultural historian Richard Tarnas describes how the societal developments of successive recent generations have brought forward and blended together new impulses for our time, culminating as a collective "call for not only an *awakening* to the spiritual and archetypal dimensions of being, but an awakening to a new *relationship* to those dimensions of being—radically participatory, co-creative, pluralistic, and dialogical." The ideal this calling invokes, writes Tarnas, is "at once unitive and pluralistic, emancipatory and relational, socially engaged and spiritually informed, embodied and ensouled."[8]

As social mystics, we accept this calling. We enact greater intimacy and awareness, making the fulfillment of Tarnas's ideal more possible for all.

Transparent communication is fundamentally an experiential and emergent practice; it allows us to create more space and deeper presence for novel future unfolding. The future is subtler than current experience; it arrives as a whisper of light. Great masters practiced cultivating a state of openness and receptivity to that field of higher coherence or super-coherence by making space for the fluid emergence of future wisdom to appear. By living out our spiritual practices while still fully engaged with one another *and* with contemporary culture, the rational disengagement and clinical distance that have been prized in modern times give way to more mutual and participatory realization and unfolding. We find that we as individuals and as communities are profoundly transformed.

When an airplane begins approaching the speed of sound, it experiences heightened drag and turbulence. Just before it cracks the sonic barrier, there's increased vibration and greater resistance. The ride gets *very* bumpy. In our present state of evolutionary development, you might say that we are flying just beneath the sound barrier of consciousness. Below that barrier, we experience greater latency: more projection, transference, dissociation, repression, and sublimation—more separation. Many of us are called to surpass the barrier, generating powerful shock waves as we do.

On the other side of the sonic *boom*, we discover heightened connection, transparency, integration, and resonance—more unity. As with any discovery, once one person and then a few more achieve an innovation in consciousness, the door swings wide for others to follow.

People all over the world are experiencing decidedly tumultuous times. Perhaps this is a sign that, collectively speaking, we're moving closer to the "speed of sound"—closer to new consciousness. Of course, the faster we travel, the more volatility we meet—until we have breached the membrane and exceeded previous evolutionary limitations. What a beautiful *boom* that will make.

PRACTICE: RELATIONAL ATTUNEMENT

Transparent communication is simply about attunement. Attuning to a person, group, organization, or even a part of your broader culture means coming into resonance by listening mindfully to the inner sensations, feelings, images, and information that arise as you tune in. Attuned relation connects you to the data flow of your own body so that you become aware of the information it receives from the other person or group.

To begin relational attunement, ground yourself in the body, simply by focusing your awareness on the body and engaging with the Three-Sync Practice that follows.

Notice the parts of your body that feel open and flowing and the parts that feel tense, numb, or absent. Simply notice whatever sensations are present.

Once you feel tuned in to the body, mindfully open yourself to the other person you want to tune in with. As you take in the other person, stay mindful of your body and how it feels. Attunement allows your body to register sensations about the other person.

As you tune in, where does the body feel open and flowing? And where does it feel tighter or more absent?

See if you can notice the emotional flavor the other person transmits. Do you sense a feeling of stress or agitation coming from them? Or do they feel relaxed, warm, and open?

Now see if you can observe the mental state of the other person. Does their mind feel busy and active, relaxed and open, curious or shut down? Simply notice whatever is present.

How does the relational or intersubjective space between you feel? Is there a sense of relaxation and connection, or do you notice a quality of distance, tension, or perhaps emptiness? The object is simply to become more attuned and more aware of whatever is present, just as it is.

You can engage in an attunement practice anytime—whenever you find yourself in a conversation or in a meeting with a group of people. At the beginning, this practice asks for patience; it might take time before you start to notice deeper perceptions. Attunement is simply your nervous system feeling and becoming aware of another's nervous system or the collective nervous system.

The more you practice, the more you will notice a deeper quality of resonance. This creates a mutual space of coherence, which is different from always feeling harmonious. By engaging in regular attunement, you're training and strengthening your inner relational capacities—and this is immeasurably helpful. For example, by staying connected and attuned *as* you communicate, you can learn to sense how deeply or well your words land in the other person.

In this way, relating becomes a dance. Sometimes the dance is easy; other times it will feel more challenging. But as you grow your capacity for attunement, the dance becomes more refined, intuitive, and inspirational. You'll soon be surprised how much you can pick up from your dance partners.

5

Presencing the Shadow

The room was very quiet with that familiar deepening that arrives
when something is happening underneath, beyond the words.
—BONNIE BADENOCH

We live in a relational universe.
Everything is relationships.
—KEITH WITT

E very aspect of our experience that remains hidden from conscious view or is unacknowledged, buried, or denied, exists in the realm of the unconscious, or the shadow. Unresolved patterns loop back through our experience again and again, taking one form or another so that they may finally be noticed and set to right. Until this happens, any unprocessed fear, shame, numbness, or other shards of the past will repeatedly obscure the present moment. Instead of seeing through the light of presence, we see through the clouded past, as if through a darkened lens. Without inner/outer coherence, there is a feeling of distance and separation, disconnection from that which is otherwise intimate and *here*.

Light is pure information in movement; the intimacy of true presence is unobstructed light. Unmet trauma reduces light by creating a "shade," or shadow, where light (life force) gets diverted into the unconscious. When the inner landscape is shaded by the ghosts of the past, the external environment is likewise occluded. The shadow hides our shame, our fears, and our traumas, but it likewise obscures our gold—our most luminous, untapped potential that includes unawakened capacities for higher orders of being and becoming. As we work to acknowledge and heal the shadow, the energies that were diverted and trapped there get released, and new potentials become clear to us.

There is no distinct or separate personal shadow; there is only shadow in the context of relationships.

Awareness-based practices, like transparent communication, teach us to be present with those parts of our nature that are hidden from our own ordinary notice—the unconscious or shadow self. As we do the work, we quickly discover that the shadow appears to us only through our interactions and relationships with others. Indeed, there *is* no distinct or separate personal shadow; there is only shadow in the context of relationships. Dimensions of shadow can be interpersonal, familial, ancestral, and cultural.

SHADOW AS A PARTICIPATORY PROCESS

You've likely observed two people who were attempting to communicate but somehow failed to see or feel one another. Instead of *commune*-icating, they merely "talked at" each other. Perhaps the overassertive energy of one person was quickly countered by a kind of guarding or walling off in the other, and vice versa. We've all participated in exchanges like this and may have come away feeling frustrated, conflicted, apathetic, or even contemptuous. No one felt heard or seen, and nothing was resolved.

Transparent communication is a method of conscious relationality that starts always with personal witness. As you speak with someone, practice noticing how much you and the other person are actually making contact. Ask yourself: *How grounded and embodied am I feeling when the conversation starts and as it continues? How much spaciousness am I experiencing? What is my current stress level? Am I able to rest in my body as I talk and listen? What am I experiencing from the other person as they speak or listen? What am I experiencing from them as* I *speak and listen?* A process of inner inquiry leads us deeper into personal contact and, therefore, deeper connection with others.

Imagine you're about to have a difficult conversation with your partner. Before the discussion even starts, you notice that you're feeling somewhat contracted. No need to judge it or change it; just notice. Does this contraction soften or harden over the course of the conversation? How does your partner's energy feel in relation to yours? What is your emotional experience? Can you name the emotions you're feeling, or do you feel numb (perhaps from prior overwhelm)? Maybe you notice a feeling of tension in your solar plexus or feel a slight headache coming on. Bodily tension is the feeling of unrestored, compressed, postponed experience, and it's often a sign that you're suppressing emotion(s). A lot of the healing you do is simply about restoring the energies that are bound up as tension or contraction back into the body to be used.

As you practice observing the subtle energies that arise and change through the process of relating, you start to discover patterns. Consider the following example.

As a child, Johann experienced parental hostility and occasional violence. To protect himself, he contracted his energy field, withdrawing access to his interior self as much as possible. This contraction helped young Johann survive the difficulty and dangers of his early experience and was, therefore, an intelligent evolutionary response of the nervous system.

As an adult, however, Johann remains contracted, withdrawn, and guarded from others, even from those whose presence might otherwise be safe and nurturing. For the most part, Johann is unaware of his aversion to connection (shadow) and simply believes that people are untrustworthy. But his long-standing pattern of withdrawal and guardedness has become maladaptive, greatly hindering Johann's ability to relate with others and, therefore, limiting his capacity to flourish.

What had once been a functional and adaptive response has now become a frozen, rigid, and dysfunctional pattern. It will likely cause Johann to feel isolated, unseen, or unrecognized by others.

As adults, it becomes our responsibility to tend to the shadow (shadow work)—to care for and liberate the frozen energies of the self that have been trapped there. There is no way to "get rid of" shadow patterns without a willingness to *go into* the pattern—to be in it with an intention to notice, witness, and feel whatever is present. We might ask ourselves: *What is my relationship to the energetic patterns that I observe in myself? What is my relationship to the blockages and difficulties that come up (e.g., do I see myself/others/the world through the lens of scarcity, criticism, or doubt)? How do I describe these subtle experiences to myself?* This kind of self-inquiry is part of a process of bringing shadow into light—inviting what has been latent and unseen to become transparent through awareness.

As you learn to presence the relational field without resistance or judgment—or, rather, with a willingness to be present with resistance or judgment—you become more aware, more awake, and less bound by shadow patterns.

The subtle field—the information available all around and within us that is accessible to us through less direct means than the blatantly material—always contains information about the shadow. When you sit across from your romantic partner or spend time with your children, the field offers a mirror in which you might observe your shadows. During work meetings, the relational field hosts information about those things that undergird the group's dynamics, allowing you to notice unspoken emotions and latent biases, motivations, or agendas. As you learn to presence the relational field without resistance or judgment—or, rather, with a willingness to be present with resistance or judgment—you become more aware, more awake, and less bound by shadow patterns.

FROM SHADOW, SEPARATION

When left to grow unchecked, shadow creates a world of disrelation, one dominated by the prevailing sense of separateness we feel and the polarization and disunity we experience all around us—a condition we have learned to see as "normal" and "just the way things are." Shadow is the pervasive architectural "substance" on which modern societies are built and through which they operate. It is the lens through which we see and with which we create our understanding. Case in point: much of what we think of as Western civilization emerged from the premise of separation, the predominant worldview that focuses on differences and distinctions: the particularities that set us, our ideas, and our environment apart.

Nearly two thousand years after Aristotle, French philosopher René Descartes cemented the worldview of separation with his proposition of dualism: that the mind and body exist as ontologically distinct phenomena. Mind-body dualism was rooted in the assumption that the human mind is wholly nonphysical, whereas the human body is entirely material. Thus, mind and body are discrete entities. The whole of modern science took to Descartes's Enlightenment philosophy, delivering us here in the twenty-first century where the preponderant view is still that the planet and the people on it are strictly physical, material wholes: individual, separate, and distinct.

In separation, the needs and desires of the individual supersede the health of larger collectives; parts override wholes. You are you, and I am me, and although we may occasionally interact, we often struggle to connect. We see the world as entirely exterior to us, a vast amalgam of bounded objects and disparate parts.

Of course, dualism may well have paved the way for many scientific, technological, and industrial advances, expanding human lifespans and generally improving the quality thereof. The advantages of modern life are undeniable. Still, we have paid a price in our unquestioning adherence to dualism and the consciousness of separation. While modern technological advancements connect us in ways previously unimagined, true connection and sustained relation remain difficult, tenuous, or simply out of reach. And this has greatly impacted our world.

Separation consciousness seems to have its own strange gravity, perpetually pulling us apart, as evidenced by the widespread phenomena of fractured families, social unrest, ongoing international conflict, hypercommercialism, and accelerating climate chaos. Ecologist Christopher Uhl describes it well:

> Pick any environmental or social problem: climate change, species extinction, environmentally linked cancers, ocean acidification, war, aquifer depletion, genocide, deforestation, loss of soil capital, coral reef decline, and in every case it is separation—the severing of relationships—that is at the root of the problem.[1]

Dualism was never the problem, however. Even atomistic individualism has been an important step in our evolutionary journey, as humankind moved from prerational tribalism to agrarian feudalism to the rise of the industrial nation-state and toward the mass-informational societies in which we find ourselves today. Despite how convenient, efficient, or even dazzling modern life can be, many people remain largely divided from their own natures and alienated from one another, adhering without question to what Otto Scharmer, MIT lecturer and co-founder of the Presencing Institute, calls "ego-system awareness." So, what can we do to change it?

SHARED RESPONSE-ABILITY TO INTEGRATE SHADOW

After the Holocaust during World War II, survivors and countless millions were unable to fully process or digest the horror that had occurred. As a result, mass unresolved material lingers, a dense and frozen plane of residual energy that can still be felt in Germany, Israel, and elsewhere. The trauma of the Holocaust produced a great transgenerational shadow, and its impacts are still felt by the descendants of survivors, soldiers, and ordinary citizens. We've seen the resurgence of this unre-solved history playing out in hyperpartisan politics and everyday life across the world, where unresolved energies are perpetually repeated in myriad forms. The untended past possesses density and opacity; it darkens the field, deepens separation, fragments communities, and delays societal development.

Even so, these unconscious patterns aren't of themselves inher-ently bad or wrong. Shadow is simply a signpost, pointing to where the lights have gone out in the system—places of disunity, rigidity, and chaos. Shadow isn't a threat to be eliminated or even a block to be removed; it is simply a reminder of what needs tending. (In fact, the unexamined instinct to "rid" ourselves of any feeling, emotion, or experience may be part of the maladaptive response that turns shadow into pathology.) Shadow is a communal defense mechanism and an evolution-ary function of the collective psyche—it holds back the tide to prevent us from drowning in overwhelm until we have the opportunity to digest and metabolize our experiences. For this reason, we must do our work to own and integrate shadow carefully and skillfully so that the burden of the past is not further postponed and passed on to future generations.

The path demands humility: it isn't that others need to be more conscious so that we can keep growing; it's that the process of growth will always challenge us to hold ourselves and others with greater care and consciousness.

By resisting the tests presented by growth—refusing to face the challenges of the present or the difficulties of the past—we forestall our spiritual development, putting the brakes on evolution. Instead of furthering our awakening, we regress. As the late Jungian analyst and author Edward Edinger advised, "Whenever one finds himself in a state of conflict with someone or with a situation, he should entertain the hypothesis that the psyche has propelled him into that situation in order to generate consciousness."[2] Each challenge presents a vital opportunity to stay related to the whole—to past, present, and future—through attunement and embodied presence. The path demands humility: it isn't that others need to be more conscious so that we can keep growing; it's that the process of growth will always challenge us to hold ourselves and others with greater care and consciousness. And this is the high art of a mystical life.

ACCESSING TRANSPERSONAL AWARENESS

As Buddhist philosophers tell us, there is only dependent origination, or *interdependent co-arising*, a philosophy that expresses how everything in existence is fundamentally interconnected—all phenomena arise in relation to other phenomena. Despite the predominance of separation consciousness, profound states of unity are possible—perhaps even evolutionarily probable. We can experience the beauty of autonomy *and* the fullness of communion, awakening into the broader field of consciousness we share.

To sustain this realization, we must develop a mature transpersonal perspective, in which one's sense of identity or experience extends beyond the personal ego to encompass greater levels of we-ness (e.g., as belonging to humankind, the planet, the cosmos, etc.). As Marcie Boucouvalas, PhD, professor emerita of human development at Virginia Polytechnic Institute, writes, "From a transpersonal perspective, humankind and the related maturation process of individuals, groups, organizations, societies, and cultures includes a balance between a separate self-sense and a deeper, broader sense of self that is 'connected.'"[3]

MATURITY AND TRANSPERSONAL PERSPECTIVE

Attaining transpersonal perspective requires maturity and an ongoing commitment to personal and relational growth. Beena Sharma, founder and president of the Center for Leadership Maturity, breaks down three critical markers of human "maturity" in this way:

1. Maturity means being able to embrace tensions, polarities, and paradoxes.

2. Maturity means getting closer to "reality" and moving in the direction of what is difficult.

3. Maturity means continuously providing feedback to self, other, and system to enable ongoing unfolding and growth.[4]

Interdependence is intrinsic; you are *also* part of a collective ecosystem, and your state of health is determined by the health of the system, just as the system's overall health is impacted by you. Transpersonal awareness clears the fog of separation, allowing us to awaken to the state of *interbeing* that visionary Buddhist monk Thich Nhat Hanh described. Of course, in order to arrive at sustained, healthy relation, there are a great many things buried in the human shadow that we must confront, acknowledge, and work to integrate, both personally and collectively. This is our collective shadow work, and only by attuning more deeply to ourselves and others can we begin it.

DISSOLVING SEPARATION

As you consider the relational capacities more deeply, including the ability to presence and host others within, you may arrive back at more fundamental questions: *Where is it that you exist? In the brain? In the body?* How is it possible to feel deeply connected to people and places that are physically quite far away? Many people report experiences in which they knew precisely the moment that a loved one had suffered an accident or even died. They simply felt it and knew. What space did the self occupy then?

In waking consciousness, you primarily perceive the material plane, but you exist as much more than your atoms. When you and I relate, our nervous systems link and connect, occupying a shared field, an informational space that is nonlinear, nonlocal, and much more than the sum of our parts. Together, we activate what we might call our *collective nervous system*, something we can sense between people in a relationship, family, community, or culture as they consciously host one another within. It is a shared and reciprocal sense of indwelling presence—of interbeing—that is our birthright as humans.

When we embark on a journey of shared healing and development, we discover the power of collective intelligence. Collective intelligence is not merely the static sum of the available capacities of each individual in the group; it is an emergent, dynamic, and fluid exchange between both the active and the potential capacities of the group and the larger social environment. By practicing exercises like those shared throughout this book, we can gain a greater sense of relational trust and develop an astonishing new sense of ourselves as belonging to a larger community of capable and creative beings. Profound possibilities for collective healing become accessible so that we discover new ways to restore the fragmentation that resides in our collective nervous system and come to know ourselves through mutual, conscious reflections with and within one another.

Far too often, we feel isolated, separate, and alone—like stranded children wandering blind in the desert. In truth, we are always and already interconnected. My shadow cannot exist without your shadow, just as your trauma cannot exist without others to initiate, share, and reinforce it. As we have seen, the fundamental damage done by trauma is the injury it creates in one's felt sense of relation to others. It causes persons, families, communities, and cultures to withdraw, distance, and numb out—to disrelate. But like walking together into a dark, mysterious cave and turning on the lights, we can bring the wider social field into consciousness. As we allow ourselves to notice previously hidden points of relation, the experience of connectedness is heightened. And we discover a new world of possibility: the communal healing field, in which one person's more integrated nervous system helps to balance the more fragmented nervous system of another. In this way, we unlock potentials for greater co-regulation and coherence.

Healing happens when you decide not to look away but to attune: to be present with what is, to notice and sense and feel. By practicing presence and attunement, you begin to discover a deeper sense of relation—to yourself and others, to your life, to the cosmos itself. This is sacred ground, where fragments are reincorporated, separation is dissolved, and greater wholeness is realized.

PRACTICE: PROCESSING THE KARMA OF THE DAY

I recommend making a regular practice of sitting down in the evenings to consciously rewind the events of the day. As you think about whatever occurred, tune in to the sensations in your body and witness whatever thoughts arise. The purpose of this practice is to consciously process the day's experiences so that your internal reactions to those experiences don't become buried, hidden, or otherwise converted into unconscious karmic (shadow) processes.

Perhaps you'd been replaying an earlier conversation over and over, regretting something you said or wishing you had made yourself clearer. Take notice when your thoughts seem to be on hyperdrive, and sense the way your body can feel less grounded, less present. Perhaps you observe a kind of buzzing sensation around the head or a busy energy above the shoulders, while everything below mid-chest feels less alive, less connected. Instead of distancing yourself from these sensations by deciding that certain feelings or thoughts "shouldn't" be present, simply rest and listen to what these thoughts, feelings, and sensations are telling you.

By making space for whatever is present, you begin to support a more emergent way of being. This strengthens your capacity to relate to life with moment-to-moment awareness, from your most essential energy or authentic core. As you undertake this path, you will also become more conscious of your inner shadow dynamics, which will allow you to integrate and heal these patterns instead of perpetually dissociating and, therefore, reinforcing them.

EMPATHY AS ANTIDOTE

The idea of sympathy—usually in the form of feeling pity for someone else—is in itself an illusion of distance, of separation. *Although I haven't personally suffered a loss, you have, and I can imagine that you must feel very sad. So, I offer you sympathy and well wishes.* Empathy, on the other hand, is a conscious remembrance of one's own experience with grief and loss so as to better resonate and relate with others in their pain. To have sympathy is to feel *for* someone (again, usually pity but occasionally also happiness), while empathetic relation is about feeling *with* others, residing in deep resonance to the other because one's interior and exterior are well connected or in sync.

I often get the question: *How do I protect myself from taking on other people's "stuff"?* People everywhere seem to be looking for an answer to this puzzling question. In contemporary vernacular, the word *empath* is often seen as someone who struggles with what we might call "leaky emotional syndrome," the problem of experiencing other people's energies and confusing them with their own or simply feeling overwhelmed by others' emotions. Some people may, in fact, have a higher degree of sensitivity, and they may suffer in this way. However, it's usually not high sensitivity but a lack of groundedness and embodiment that causes the overwhelm—often rooted in attachment injuries. Healing the root trauma creates a more stable sense of embodiment, which allows a person to experience their high sensitivity as a gift rather than a curse. We might think of it like a tree with a very large crown of branches; it needs equally strong roots to stand.

Again, it isn't that we have somehow absorbed or taken on another person's emotions like human sponges with no barriers or boundaries, but that, somewhere within us—perhaps in a place that is hidden to us—we are in resonance with the unmet emotional energies or frozen experiences of the other. Like a piano string to a tuning fork, we feel ourselves vibrating in sympathetic resonance to the rhythms brought by their presence. It isn't just the other person's emotions that we're feeling, but also our own. Instead of trying to protect ourselves from other people's energy, we could choose to explore with curiosity the resonance between our inner wounds and theirs.

The challenge is not how to protect against, avoid, or ward off the overwhelming emotions we feel from others, it's how to stay present with others when difficult emotions arise so that we might assist in the co-regulation of intense energies—for their benefit and for ours. Emotional regulation makes digestion and integration possible, so difficult feelings can be fully processed and resolved. And this brings us back into relation.

ILLUMINATING THE FIELD

Recently, researchers in the fields of social cognitive neuroscience and the philosophy of mind have begun witnessing something that many contemplatives have long sensed, which supports the idea of the collective shadow. In their work, the *extended mind theory* (EMT) proposes that the human mind is not limited to the boundaries of the brain or even the body but extends into its environment. For example, the painting you've been working on, your personal diary, and even your smartphone or laptop are infused with your mind and, as such, are part of your cognitive process.[5]

More arresting is how EMT connects to emerging theories of social cognition. Researchers are looking at how two or more brains (and, therefore, minds) can synchronize or "couple," such as in instances of shared intention or cooperative action. An "extended social mind" emerges when multiple brains (and, thus, multiple central nervous systems) link together in a highly coherent fashion. Consciousness researchers Ana Lucía Valencia and Tom Froese write:

> The association between neural oscillations and functional integration is widely recognized in the study of human cognition. Large-scale synchronization of neural activity has also been proposed as the neural basis of consciousness. Intriguingly, a growing number of studies in social cognitive neuroscience reveal that phase synchronization similarly appears across brains during meaningful social interaction. Moreover, this inter-brain synchronization has been associated with subjective reports of social connectedness, engagement, and cooperativeness, as well as experiences of social cohesion and self-other merging. These findings challenge the standard view of human consciousness as essentially first-person singular and private.[6]

Researchers argue that evidence of "inter-brain synchronization in the fastest frequency bands" may profoundly transform our understanding of human consciousness. As we consider these scientific insights in light of what we know of trauma or toxic stress, it's possible to sense into a bright, flourishing new world of possibility for humanity—or as Charles Eisenstein's book title conveys, "the more beautiful world our hearts know is possible." The power of mutual witness clarifies our collective shadow, making it possible to acknowledge, own, integrate, and transcend.

What we call "we-space" awareness is created when people actively work together to presence the field. The effort and intention to generate we-space vitalizes willingness, compassion, and shared courage; amplifies attunement; and awakens our collective intelligence. The power of mutual witness clarifies our collective shadow, making it possible to acknowledge, own, integrate, and transcend.

Jorge N. Ferrer, PhD, author and former professor at the East-West Psychology Program at the California Institute of Integral Studies, proposes that transpersonal phenomena are "participatory events that can emerge in the locus of an individual, a relationship, a collective identity, or a place." Co-creative participation engages human beings in what Ferrer calls *participatory knowing,* a "multidimensional access to reality that can involve not only the creative power of the mind but also that of the body, the heart, and the soul."[7]

This is the heart of transpersonal work, a deeply *conscious* participatory process, which has the astonishing effect of accelerating human development. It's about coming together with the goal of perceiving ourselves and one another in higher resolution. This allows us to notice when there is a degree of density or shadow in the intersubjective atmosphere, and it helps us better navigate the familial and cultural shadowlands.

Astonishingly, the power of collective healing extends much deeper into reality and further across time than currently understood. As we'll explore in the chapters ahead, mutual presencing practices can help us heal the wounds of our ancestral and historical past, making new futures possible for ourselves and our descendants. This is where our true facility for interbeing is realized.

6

Trauma's Impact

There is no present or future—only the
past, happening over and over again.
—EUGENE O'NEILL

Time is being and being
time, it is all one thing,
the shining, the seeing,
the dark abounding.
—URSULA K. LE GUIN

n her remarkable book, *Black Hole Survival Guide*, astrophysicist Janna Levin offers a poetic description of a nearly impossible-to-fathom phenomenon:

When in pursuit of a black hole, you are not looking for a material object. A black hole can masquerade as an object, but it is really a place—a place in space and time. Better: a black hole is a spacetime.

Shed the impression of the black hole as a dense crush of matter. Accept the black hole as a bare event horizon; a curved, empty spacetime; a sparse vacuity . . . A glorious void, an empty venue, an extreme, spare stage—markedly austere but, yes, able to support big drama when the stage is occupied. Black holes are a place in space, and they barricade their secrets. [1]

Another difficult-to-fathom phenomenon is the one we call "trauma" (a.k.a., karma or shadow). Like the astrophysicist's black hole, trauma can be sensed as an absence or nothingness that barricades its secrets and, however strange, has a distinct location in space and time.

Although a person's past traumatic experiences are often invisible—secrets never to be revealed—they simultaneously exist as a great density of energy, powerful enough to disfigure the very fabric of reality. The closer we get to one of these traumatized zones, the stranger things appear. And yet, all too often, we take this strangeness on as "normal"—just the way things are. Like the supermassive black hole at the center of our galaxy, unmet traumas are powerful phenomena; they can eventually come to consume us. To escape the magnificent gravity of a traumatic black hole, or what Holocaust survivor Primo Levi described as a "grey and turbid nothing," we must come to understand the physics that rule them.

In the dark winter of 1944, Levi found himself packed with 649 other Italian Jews onto cattle trucks bound for the concentration camps in occupied Poland. A brilliant writer and chemist, he endured eleven months at Auschwitz, seven more than anyone was expected to survive, before the camp was finally liberated by the Red Army in January of 1945. Levi was one of only twenty or so Italians in his original transport who left there alive. [2]

The atrocities Levi endured in Auschwitz were unspeakable. Still, the shy, bookish chemist eventually went on to write of his experiences in detail, offering the world an intricate account of the human-on-human barbarity he'd witnessed and suffered firsthand. In the decades after, Levi's work made him a heroic figure in the public imagination—and, certainly, he was. Yet, for all his endurance, wisdom, and virtuosity, in 1987, Levi lost his life in a three-story fall at his home in Turin, Italy;

his death was officially ruled a suicide. Despite an unbelievable legacy of survival and the brilliant, deeply inspiring work he produced before his death, Primo Levi had remained plagued by unrelenting depression and traumatic memories that overwhelmed his essential resilience and eventually his will to live.

In the conclusion of his book, *The Truce* (published in English as *The Reawakening*), Levi writes:

> [And] a dream full of horror has still not ceased to visit me, at sometimes frequent, sometimes longer, intervals. It is a dream within a dream, varied in detail, one in substance. I am sitting at a table with my family, or with friends, or at work, or in the green countryside; in short, in a peaceful, relaxed environment, apparently without tension or affliction; yet I feel a deep and subtle anguish, the definite sensation of an impending threat. And in fact, as the dream proceeds slowly and brutally, each time in a different way, everything collapses and disintegrates around me, the scenery, the walls, the people, while the anguish becomes more intense and more precise. Now everything has changed into chaos; I am alone in the center of a grey and turbid nothing, and now I know what this thing means, and I also know that I have always known it; I am in the *Lager* once more, and nothing is true outside the *Lager*.[3]

After news of Levi's death, Elie Wiesel, author, Nobel laureate, and fellow Holocaust survivor, made a poignant and painful observation: "Primo Levi died at Auschwitz, forty years later."[4] American writer William Faulkner spoke truth when he wrote, "The past is never dead. It's not even past."[5]

Perhaps the most debilitating legacy of unhealed trauma is the damage it does to our ability to relate to one another or even to feel embodied and connected to ourselves. Some traumas, whether personal or collective, are so catastrophic in nature—human-on-human traumas, in particular—that it is difficult, some say impossible, to pass their event horizon and remain intact. Eventually, they devour us. There is nevertheless an evolutionary intelligence inherent in our responses to great adversity that makes it possible to survive, adapt, and transform even the worst of our suffering. And with care and patience, presence and attunement, we can utilize what we learn from trauma to repair ourselves and the broken connections between us.

In my 2020 book, *Healing Collective Trauma: A Process for Integrating Our Intergenerational and Cultural Wounds*, I address the subject of trauma at length and in much greater detail. However, for the purposes of deepening our examination of relational wisdom, let us proceed with a condensed overview.

TRAUMA DEFINED

Whether or not you have personally experienced psychological trauma, you are likely familiar with its visage: in literature, film, television, or by virtue of knowing someone who has undergone intense adversity and struggles in some way as a result.

From the modern psychiatric perspective, trauma is a psychological and potentially developmental injury caused by an overwhelming experience or experiences. According to the Perelman School of Medicine at the University of Pennsylvania, "Psychological trauma is caused by an adverse experience, or series of experiences, that results in an injury that changes the way the brain functions, impairing neurophysiological, psychological, and cognitive functioning."[6] In plainer words, trauma changes us.

Peter A. Levine, PhD, American clinical psychologist and author, defines trauma as the "debilitating symptoms people experience in the aftermath of *perceived* life-threatening or overwhelming experiences." We become traumatized, says Levine, "when our ability to respond to a perceived threat is in some way overwhelmed." In *Healing Trauma*, he writes that trauma is the "most avoided, ignored, denied, misunderstood, and untreated cause of human suffering."[7]

For our purposes, the word *trauma* does not refer to the adversity that engenders suffering, but rather to the individual or group's *response* to that adversity. Trauma is what happens inside us, at the level of the nervous system, due to the adverse experience. Much like a black hole, it is difficult to observe the presence of psychological trauma with the naked eye; we can detect it only by its effects: the telltale symptoms it produces in persons or communities.

A NEUROPSYCHOLOGICAL PERSPECTIVE ON TRAUMA

The human central nervous system employs an ancient, evolutionary response to any acute stressor or potentially life-threatening event. As with other animals, an encounter with a perceived threat automatically engages a fight, flight, or freeze reaction via the sympathetic nervous system. In short, the body gears up to do battle, run away, or play dead.

In a sense, fleeing and freezing are both forms of disappearing. Certain reptiles, amphibians, marine animals, and even insects are able to vanish into their surroundings with an instantaneous, camouflaging color change. (As defense mechanisms go, "invisibility" is a neat trick.) For humans, disappearance can take the form of dissociation—emotional detachment from one's surroundings—or a more serious disconnection from the sensory and emotional experiences of the body. If unable to flee from potential attack, we frequently flee from ourselves.

Whatever response one's nervous system selects, there is an instant and automatic biophysical reaction. A cascade of stress hormones—cortisol, adrenaline, and norepinephrine—elicits a rise in heart rate and blood pressure, all the better for running or fighting. An encounter with an intense stressor brings the brain and body into a state of hyperarousal, in which the stressed person becomes unusually attentive, anxious, and alert, or into a state of shutdown, or freezing in place.

These are all adaptive responses intended to support survival in the short term. But after a threatening incident has passed, it can sometimes be difficult for the brain and body to find the shutoff valve.

Even when a threat is long gone, the body may continue to respond as if it were in ever-present danger. If the stress response becomes unusually prolonged in this way, the extremes of hyperarousal or shutdown can become fixed, rigid, and repetitive, and, therefore, maladaptive to the life of the traumatized individual.

Consider the symptoms: prolonged hyperarousal can manifest as hypervigilance, heightened reactivity, irritability, anger, aggression, increased anxiety, panic, and the ensuing problems these can cause, such as chronic inattentiveness and difficulty sleeping. On the other end of the spectrum, persistent shutdown can produce flat or constricted affect, emotional blunting, hopelessness, numbness, indifference, apathy, lethargy, detachment, and dissociation. "If hyperarousal is the nervous system's accelerator," writes Levine, "a sense of overwhelming helplessness is its brake. The helplessness that is experienced at such times is not the ordinary sense of helplessness that can affect anyone from time to time. It is the sense of being collapsed, immobilized, and utterly helpless. It is not a perception, belief, or a trick of the imagination. It is real."[8]

These and other symptoms of unresolved trauma appear as a continuum of extremes, experienced by people and by societies. We need only look around to observe their overwhelming presence in our world.

We might divide these symptoms into three general categories:

1. hyperactivation and stress

2. numbness and detachment

3. fragmentation and separation

Everyone who has ever been traumatized has experienced a moment when "being here" wasn't a safe option. The psychological defense mechanisms (i.e., symptoms) that followed as a result were an intelligent way of dealing with that. Being present is only possible for the healthy, integrated parts of oneself. The traumatized parts simply can't be present because being present isn't a safe option.

In contemporary society where the concept of psychological pathology reigns, people can become hyperconcerned about perceived areas of deficiency, weakness, and potential dysfunction. But many seeming dysfunctions were originally adaptive strategies for survival that have simply run their course. It is time to collectively reframe the deficit-based image of what it means to be human. Most of us want to be "better" or more developed, so we set out to vanquish the parts of ourselves that seem to cause our suffering. But we can never remove a part of ourselves, and the desire to do so merely reproduces the originating trauma. We can't get rid of the injured pieces of our own soul, but we can meet and integrate those places within us—and in so doing, expand our inner-world space, deepen our perspective, and revive our latent capacity to relate more deeply to others.

It is time to collectively reframe the deficit-based image of what it means to be human.

TYPES OF TRAUMA

A healthy, well-regulated nervous system can go through periods of creative stress and high performance and return to rest and regeneration. The traumatized nervous system is unable to self-regulate and is often operating under toxic stress. Broadly speaking, there are three types of trauma. Most people are familiar with the first two:

Acute trauma results from a single adverse incident, such as an accident, illness or injury, sexual assault, natural disaster, or from witnessing or experiencing an act of violence.

Chronic trauma results from ongoing or repeated traumas, such as domestic violence, emotional abuse, sexual abuse, repeated bullying, or coercion and control.

An important example of chronic trauma is known as *complex trauma*, also referred to as *early relational trauma, developmental trauma,* or *attachment trauma*. It occurs as the result of ongoing childhood or adolescent adversity, such as emotional, physical, or sexual abuse; emotional, physical, or medical neglect; and abandonment. Complex trauma is particularly insidious as it is known to inhibit, delay, or injure the natural developmental process. Complex trauma can, thus, harm a child's self-concept, behavior, cognition, long-term health, future orientation, and economic outcomes through adulthood.[9]

Trauma researchers and clinicians frequently remark on the conspiracy of silence that pervades circumstances of ongoing child abuse and neglect, in which witting family members and community members implicitly or unconsciously agree to keep quiet about the abuse, neglect, or incest, and they rarely confront an abuser or intervene on the child's behalf. Some have described this as the "traumatic atmosphere," referring to the "everyday climate, which can be highly destructive to the Self" of an abused or neglected child.[10]

German psychoanalyst Werner Bohleber, PhD, defines *trauma* as "a brute fact that cannot be integrated into a context of meaning at the time it is experienced because it tears the fabric of the psyche," and refers to the "reluctance to know" on the part of traumatized persons, families, and society at large.[11] This reluctance to witness, know of, or intercede on behalf of victims is deeply and powerfully embedded in the complex of relational trauma. Humans disown, deny, avoid, and suppress what they cannot bear to acknowledge.

Complex trauma is now known to have a deleterious impact on the psychological development of the growing child or adolescent and is strongly linked to a higher incidence of mental and physical illness later in life. A groundbreaking 1995 study conducted by the Centers for Disease Control and Kaiser Permanente examined the impact of Adverse Childhood Experiences (ACEs) over a lifespan. (ACEs include abuse, neglect, and a dysfunctional family environment—e.g., having a parent or primary caregiver with a mental illness or addiction, or growing up with an incarcerated parent.)

Since the original 1995 study, dozens more have been conducted on ACEs, and those studies reveal the existence of a "powerful, persistent correlation" between the number of ACEs experienced by the child and poor outcomes later in life, according to a Harvard University report on ACEs and toxic stress. These outcomes include "dramatically increased risk of heart disease, diabetes, obesity, depression, substance abuse, smoking, poor academic achievement, time out of work, and early death." The report goes on to explain:

> In the early 2000s, the National Scientific Council on the Developing Child coined the term "toxic stress" to describe extensive, scientific knowledge about the effects of excessive activation of stress response systems on a child's developing brain as well as the immune system, metabolic regulatory systems, and cardiovascular system. Experiencing ACEs triggers all of these interacting stress response systems. When a child experiences multiple ACEs over time—**especially without supportive relationships with adults to provide buffering protection**—the experiences will trigger an excessive and long-lasting stress response.[12] *[Emphasis is mine.]*

More recently, ACEs researchers have included environmental and systemic adversity to the types of toxic stress that can be injurious over the lifespan. Taken into account are collective traumas such as community violence, chronic poverty, and systemic racism. As Harvard's Center on the Developing Child explains, "The body's stress response does not distinguish between overt threats from inside or outside the home environment; it just recognizes when there is a threat and goes on high alert."[13]

ACKNOWLEDGING COLLECTIVE TRAUMA

The third type of trauma is that of collective trauma, though it goes by many other names—historical trauma, cultural trauma, racial trauma, multi- or intergenerational trauma—all of which refer to the traumatic stress experienced by a given group, community, or society. The consequences of collective trauma are frequently felt by multiple generations within a family or families.

Maria Yellow Horse Brave Heart, PhD, associate professor in the Department of Psychiatry and the director of Native American and Disparities Research at the University of New Mexico, defines *historical trauma* as the "cumulative emotional and psychological wounding over the lifespan and across generations, emanating from massive group trauma experiences," and refers in her work to the historical trauma response (HTR), which she defines as "the constellation of features in reaction to massive group trauma."

> The HTR often includes depression, self-destructive behavior, suicidal thoughts and gestures, anxiety, low self-esteem, anger, and difficulty recognizing and expressing emotions. It may include substance abuse, often an attempt to avoid painful feelings through self-medication. Historical unresolved grief is the associated affect that accompanies HTR; this grief may be considered fixated, impaired, delayed, and/or disenfranchised.[14]

Yellow Horse Brave Heart has undertaken a careful study of HTR among Indigenous North American populations, Japanese American internment camp survivors and descendants, and Jewish Holocaust survivors and descendants. The commonalities among groups are at once illuminating and heartbreaking, and they should be understood, especially by those seeking to impart trauma-informed care.

TRAUMATIC IMPACTS ARE PASSED DOWN

In 1966, the late Canadian psychiatrist Vivian M. Rakoff, MD, wrote one of the first papers on the subject of intergenerational trauma. In his study, he noted the unusually high prevalence of psychological distress among descendants of Holocaust survivors.[15] Dr. Rakoff was a researcher at the Jewish General Hospital in Montreal, a city with a large population of Holocaust survivors. In the half-century since that study was published, research into the intergenerational nature of trauma has flourished. Much of that research looks into the mental-health outcomes—e.g., generalized anxiety, depression, substance use disorders, PTSD, and suicidality—that trauma leaves behind for families and communities of all types.

Another area of research focuses on the epigenetic effects underlying the transmission of transgenerational trauma. The term *epigenetic* refers to heritable changes to DNA that are caused by environmental influences and affect how genes are expressed without altering the DNA sequence.

Dr. Isabelle Mansuy, professor of neuroepigenetics at the University of Zürich, conducts ongoing research into the mechanisms of epigenetic inheritance as it relates to childhood trauma. In 2001, Mansuy designed a mice study using an intervention intended to re-create conditions of childhood trauma. The researchers separated mice pups from their mothers at unpredictable intervals and employed other stressors—such as placing the mothers in water or a confined space—before reuniting the mothers with their offspring. In mice that were exposed to these stressful experiences, the researchers observed a pattern of posttraumatic stress behaviors such as avoidance, increased risk-taking, increased calorie intake, and increased antisocial behavior—behaviors that are also observed in children who have been exposed to trauma.[16]

Interestingly, the same posttraumatic stress behaviors were observed in the second generation of offspring (i.e., the grandchildren) born to the original male pups, even though the second generation was not exposed to the experimental stress conditions and was not socialized with their male progenitors. (In the mouse species, males have no role in caring for the young.)

Mansuy and her team isolated an epigenetic source for the transmission. As UK journalist Martha Henriques writes, "The researchers extracted RNA molecules from the sperm of male mice who had been traumatized, and they injected these molecules into early embryos of mice whose parents had not experienced this early-life trauma. The resulting pups, however, showed the typical altered behavioral patterns of a pup whose parents experienced trauma."[17]

Perhaps our contemporary understanding of the epigenetic transmission of trauma and the complex social factors experienced by members of historically traumatized groups might illuminate in some way the ancient biblical passage in which God speaks to Moses, explaining that "the iniquity of the fathers [shall be visited] upon the children, and upon the children's children, unto the third and to the fourth generation."[18] It is not just the direct experiencers who suffer the consequences of adversity; it is also their families, their descendants, and their communities. As trauma researchers Bessel van der Kolk, Alexander C. McFarlane, and Lars Weisaeth write in their book *Traumatic Stress*:

> Despite the human capacity to survive and adapt, traumatic experiences can alter people's psychological, biological, and social equilibrium to such a degree that one particular event comes to taint all other experiences, spoiling appreciation of the present. This tyranny of the past interferes with the ability to pay attention to both new and familiar situations. When people come to concentrate selectively on reminders of their past, life tends to become colorless, and contemporary experience ceases to be a teacher.[19]

The paradox of the human response to trauma is that it is an elegant evolutionary adaptation meant to aid survival. When left to linger, however, it can eventually produce inelegant, maladaptive disintegration. We relive, again and again, the "tyranny of the past"—our own and that of our ancestors, and history ceaselessly repeats. Even if we manage to block out the past and proceed through our lives as if it never existed, "the body keeps the score," as explained in trauma researcher Van der Kolk's bestselling book of that title. Our children and our children's children will be forced to carry the weight of what we ourselves have survived but left unhealed.

Cathy Caruth, PhD, author and professor of English and Comparative Literature at Cornell University focuses on the "language of trauma and testimony," and describes "a speaking and a listening *from the site of trauma*," which does not rely "on simply what we know of each other, but what we don't yet know of our own traumatic pasts." She continues, "In a catastrophic age . . . trauma itself may provide the very link between cultures: not as a simple understanding of the pasts of others but rather . . . as our ability to listen through the departures we have all taken from ourselves."[20] In previous chapters, we explored the process of attunement to places of absence or numbness, recognizing the need to practice and hone our ability to "listen through the departures," as Caruth says.

HILORIE BAER'S PROFOUND DISCOVERY OF WHAT IS HERE

Hilorie Baer is a personal coach and transformational facilitator working with individuals, couples, and groups. She lives in Jerusalem, where she maintains a private psychotherapy practice. In an interview about ancestral and collective trauma, she said:

One of the biggest changes [in my therapeutic practice] has come through learning to understand and work with energy. The story and the information carried by the energy here [in Israel] is very dense. So, understanding energy is very important. And what is energy? Energy is alive; it's what's here.

So this kind of healing work is really about energy, the energy that's here and now and present and alive. There is energy that's present in me that comes before me. It was present in my parents' lives and their parents' lives. It's as if you're working in one room, but there are smells and noise and all kinds of stuff coming from other rooms. But if you don't know those other rooms are there, then you don't know how to work with them. They are impacting you, but you don't know it. Then, suddenly, you open up a drawer and you're like, "Oh! *That's* what that is."

Learning to work in the context of ancestral and collective trauma opened the doors to those other rooms. It opened new spaces to perceive and digest "what's happening now." [For some of my clients,] this has been life changing. Without the ancestral understanding, the ceiling is just very low. And without the language to examine the ancestral component, the client just keeps going back into their own childhood story, looking for the cause. But it isn't there.

As a therapist, learning to sense energetically when something ancestral is playing out now has opened the playing field. Jung brought in a lot of tools to help us understand this, like the Jungian archetypes and the collective unconscious. Yet most of traditional psychotherapy isn't working with that at all. But the fact is: I can't feel myself fully if I don't feel [the lineage trauma]. It's just true.

We are all in the trauma field. And what is that? It's reality! But we don't even know it's there. We don't know that trauma is there, that collective trauma is present. It's just "life." It's just "how it is." So, to feel it as trauma is the only way we begin to change the "reality" that we're in.

I've had some deeply powerful personal experiences that opened my eyes to the question of "What is here now?" In CTIP

[Collective Trauma Integration Process] groups, we'd be doing our processing work and suddenly something would just rise up. The energy of "all the other rooms," so to speak, would just be there. I was once in Germany for a group event like this, and as I was sitting in that room, I was suddenly overcome with a feeling of terror and rage. It was *in* me.

All the other people there were my friends; they were people I love. I stay at their homes. I'm part of their community, and I love being with them. But at that moment, all of that was gone and I was in a place where I literally felt: *I am going to be killed or I am going to have to kill.* It was intense, as if the curtain had just come up.

What I felt wasn't mental; it was alive. And it is always there. It wasn't created in our group; it was already present. It had just been covered over or hidden from view. And until that moment, I hadn't been in the same frequency [as that unresolved emotional energy], and no one else had been in that frequency. We were all just friends and everything was cool—very different frequency. But the moment the curtain came up, I was sick. But because this was a trusted retreat, I felt safe to speak to the group from that place, [after which the group held and processed it together].

That experience showed me that there's a lot that is here, or that's inside me, that I'm suppressing, that I'm defending against—all the time, even if I'm completely unaware of it. And I could see how all of this is also playing out in my culture and my country, in Israel, and the recognition really opened me. In Israel, everything is very political: *This is right, and this is wrong.* But all of this is beyond politics, completely. The challenge is to find other people who are willing to go inside it, to see and hold what's "behind the curtain" together. [21]

FRACTURED CONNECTION

To the extent that health can be seen as a balanced movement of free-flowing life-force energies, trauma is any response to experience that overwhelms this balance, leaving some portion of the life force blocked, trapped, or frozen, reducing the overall flow of our vital force through the system. These quanta of shuttered energy occupy real places in space and time, possessing a cosmic address. Each one holds an aspect of self that, by virtue of toxic stress, has become restricted, separated, and unreachable to the conscious self. As oblique or invisible as past traumas may seem, they are like black holes in the constellation of being. And they are not simply "personal problems," as there is no such thing as individual trauma, individual shadow, or individual karma. Each of us is an expression of the whole; we influence and are influenced by the whole.

As Clara Mucci, PhD, an author and psychoanalytically oriented psychotherapist who practices in Italy, writes, "The same dynamics that occur in the psyche [of traumatized persons] also form the collective environment."[22] No matter how much we attempt to distance ourselves from the iniquities of the world, all human suffering is shared. Every person's pain is carried by all persons.

Perhaps the greatest consequence of trauma is that it fragments and dislocates us, breaking down our capacity to relate and connect with ourselves and one another in a healthy state of interdependence. In his book *Everything in Its Path*, Kai T. Erikson explains that collective trauma is a "blow to the basic tissue of social life that damages the bonds attaching people together and impairs the prevailing sense of communality."[23] As psychologist Abraham Maslow knew, it is not enough to survive: to have adequate food, shelter, or safety. To truly thrive, humans require a sense of mutuality and belonging. Indeed, relational health is at the very heart of human well-being and is the primary engine through which we develop. If this capacity has been disrupted or severed by past adversity, we must make it our mission to repair and rebuild—as much for ourselves as for our future descendants.

As long as the shadow of collective trauma persists and accumulates, it acts to inhibit humanity's evolutionary development, suppress our potential, and prevent us from realizing a new and better future.

For these reasons, it is incumbent upon us to acknowledge and integrate the pain of the past in order to become more whole, more healed, more present.

It was once assumed that nothing escapes a black hole. Physicists termed this the "black hole information paradox," one they have been attempting to resolve for nearly half a century, and it finally appears they have, at least in theory. From *Quanta Magazine*: "Information, [theoretical physicists] now say with confidence, does escape a black hole. If you jump into one, you will not be gone for good. Particle by particle, the information needed to reconstitute your body will re-emerge."[24] It's a curiously strange idea, perhaps useful for reminding us that our dislocated fragments are never gone for good. No matter how dark or harrowing the traumas we (or our ancestors) have passed through, there is always hope that we can one day reemerge, whole and complete, our broken bonds restored through attunement, presence, and the wisdom of relation.

part two

I n part II, we'll deepen our understanding of attunement and learn how trauma can and must be healed in individuals, ancestral lines, communities, and societies. We'll explore the role of healing professionals and ordinary people in this vital work and consider the evolutionary impacts of such healing for our own lives and the fate of our world.

In places, part II is written with therapists, health-care professionals, facilitators, and healers of all kinds foremost in mind, though the information it contains can be utilized by anyone. In those sections, I recommend that the general reader imagine themselves in both the professional and the "client" role, and that they consider how the interactions or practices described might apply to their own lives and relationships.

7

The Power of Healing Relation

We may be on the verge of a massive shift in how we view
time, causality, and information. Classical causality, the one-
thing-after-another billiard-ball world of Isaac Newton and his
Enlightenment friends, is being revealed as folk causality, a cultural
construct and a belief system, not the way things really are.

—ERIC WARGO

Love is our true destiny. We do not find the meaning of
life by ourselves alone—we find it with another.

—THOMAS MERTON

Proper trauma work requires deep skill, empathy, transpersonal competence, and groundedness. To "do no harm," we as healers must be able to witness a client's—or anyone's—traumatic experiences compassionately and through a wide-enough, deep-enough lens. We must grow the eyes to see the ways a person's past, including that of their genetic or communal forebears, is still resident inside them today. How does ancestral or communal trauma show up? What are the indicators? How can we accurately presence the invisible past and come to sense what is absent, missing, or interfering with the present? These are the aims of integrated relational healing.

As we discussed in chapter 6, trauma is defined not by an external event but by the internal reaction one has to a traumatizing experience. Trauma is a response of the nervous system that becomes crystallized at the very moment in time a shock or adversity occurs, a kind of physicalized snapshot of the body-mind that is then stored in the body until it can be processed and transmuted. In this way, trauma is very much a manifestation of the past—a moment from earliest childhood, for example.

Not all of the trauma that gets encoded in your central nervous system is yours alone. Some may be rooted in adversities that were experienced by an ancestor or many ancestors, long before you were born. When a system of trauma is perpetuated for decades or even hundreds or thousands of years, its effects may be expressed by everyone born into the culture. In the history of our kind, countless traumas have been handed down from one generation to another in the form of unhealed, unintegrated energies (i.e., the crystalized past), which are now inextricable from our lives in the present.

As we have seen, this is what traumatizing experiences do: they fragment and separate our vital energy, making it difficult to be fully present in time while we are holding on to fractured, past information. When something happens to activate a fragmented trauma "file," so to speak, the nervous system becomes "triggered" or activated, and we can regress back to the stage of our development at the time the trauma first occurred (e.g., back to the five-year-old self).

Knowing in advance what might activate a person's trauma is often hard to predict, and the response itself may seem outsized or irrational to an outside observer. This is due to the fragmented nature of trauma. Because the original energy of the trauma is broken apart in the system, any correspondences or links to the whole are disconnected, making regression more likely.

And this is not an accident. In fact, even the triggers or activations of past trauma possess a kind of evolutionary brilliance. When the five-year-old's trauma occurred, a certain aspect of their development was prevented from unfolding in a healthy way and is still waiting to be released, like a wrinkle in spacetime waiting to be smoothed so that the whole film can finally play clearly. The triggered regression is like a pop-up window, prompting that release: "Warning: look at this issue!"

These fragmented files explain why, in certain areas of your life, everything seems to flow in a synchronized manner, while in other areas things can feel stuck, stagnated, or blocked. Maybe in your professional life, things generally unfold easily. You tend to meet just the right people at the right time or attract key clients or customers with ease. Yet, in your personal or romantic life, things might feel more difficult or less synchronized. That difficulty or "stuckness" may exist due to unintegrated traumas in the area of intimate relationships. There is either coherence and serendipity or incoherence, fragmentation, and desynchronization. In the event of the latter, there are signals one can look to in order to discover precisely which "files" are broken and in need of system cleanup.

So often, we struggle with fear, doubt, numbness, unease, and anxiety that overshadows "the movie," which is to say the fullest and clearest flow of light and information about our present experience: all that is happening or available to us right now. Trauma energy creates a filter over our perception; where we are traumatized, our perception of the world is distorted and limited; awareness is reduced or overshadowed. This is why we so often project our disowned trauma onto the world and react as if the trauma is still happening to us because of other people.

Genuine healing has the power to restore distortions and bring about inner and outer coherence, including improved relationships. As you heal, that broken piece belonging to your past can be brought back into the fold. Through embodied, mature awareness, you become attuned to any parts of yourself that are absent or out of sync and can consciously work to reintegrate those aspects of self.

In ordinary moments of challenge or stress—let's use the example of a difficult team meeting at work—you may feel a bit blocked or stagnated or stymied, but you can usually find your way through it. Perhaps the perceived problem arises because you're lacking in specific business knowledge or financial resources. Once you recognize what is missing and start the hunt to attain it, you begin to feel empowered again. You can now bring in the support or acquire the competencies that are needed and work your way toward a solution or resolution.

However, if the original stress arises because of an unmet prior adversity or trauma, you might be unable to sort out what is missing and needed; therefore, you might be unable to feel your agency. You may even collapse into a state of paralysis or overwhelm, so you freeze, unable to make a move. Or you might regress and react against others or out of accord with the demands of the moment. The thought *I can't do this!* will feel utterly true, as if life has suddenly commanded you to fly an airplane made of bricks and twine. Your overwhelmed reaction to the current stress, however, is much less about the stress itself than it is an activation of *prior* trauma.

Likewise, our responsibility to those with whom we engage in relationship is to learn to truly be with them in their own moments of difficulty by attuning to them as they are, where they are.

Trauma produces a feeling of scarcity, a feeling of not enough. Not enough time, not enough space, not enough resources, not enough connection or support. In Stephen Mitchell's translation of the *Tao Te Ching*, there is a beautiful line: "When the master runs into difficulties, she stops and gives herself to them."[1] Think about that for a moment. She doesn't cling to her comforts or scream out at her problems. Instead, "she stops and gives herself to them." This is a way of saying, *I need to take some space.*

When that feeling of scarcity, of "not enough" happens, the antidote is to stop—to take a moment, to take some space, some time. To be with whatever is arising internally, in order to better relate with what is happening externally. Likewise, our responsibility to those with whom we engage in relationship is to learn to truly be with them in their own moments of difficulty by attuning to them as they are, where they are. (This is also the duty of clinicians, healers, therapists, facilitators, and coaches.)

While this is a simple thing, it is not easy. So, it's important to consider what really "being with"—in other words, being present and attuned with—one another can look and feel like.

SENSING IN CONNECTION

When you and I sit down together to have a conversation, I listen to you, and you listen to me. Real listening requires a commitment to presence, of course, so we do much more than hear with our ears and comprehend with our minds. I not only hear you, I *feel* you—and I feel you feeling me. In his book, *Mindsight,* Dan Siegel describes this as "feeling felt," a connection that happens when "we sense that our internal world is shared, that our mind is *inside* the other."[2] This feeling of connection becomes a dance. There's a pulsing rhythm to our listening and speaking, receiving and contributing. And as long as we're aware of our own experience—physical, mental, and emotional—we can connect deeply with one another. And it's a beautiful dance. But if, as we talk together, something I hear or sense somehow touches a part of me that is closed off, numb, dissociated, or dissonant, that dormant feeling can rise up, and the rhythm between us is lost.

Perhaps somewhere in our conversation I become a little inflamed and reactive, or suddenly removed and distant. You will feel that. To you, I now appear defensively walled off, unable to connect with or understand you. Maybe you even notice that I now seem a little dissociated or disembodied. As we've discussed, traumatic activations tend to show up along a spectrum of extremes—from hyperarousal to hypoarousal. When my unresolved past has been activated in this way, I can no longer be present with you in our relational space; I regress, disintegrate, and detach.

This is why it's so important to be able to look, listen, and feel with the whole body, to use one's entire nervous system to tune in. With your nervous system fully engaged, you're able to pick up a lot more information about the physical, emotional, mental, and relational interplay. And this kind of whole-body listening is especially important for those who engage in healing work.

People who seek awakened connection with others—whether we are therapists, facilitators, healers, or simply practitioners—must practice the art of staying conscious and attuned with what is happening both within ourselves and within the other, fine-tuning our ability to sense coherence or incoherence in the connection.

There are many daily practices that can help us heighten our faculties for perceiving relational coherence. Broadly speaking, these practices utilize four interlinking elements: physical, emotional, mental, and relational states.

> **Physical state.** In any given moment, you can connect to the sensations of your physical body by simply opening your awareness to physical sensation or lack of sensation throughout the regions of the body. What is the pace and depth of your breath? How is your posture? As you pay attention to your body, where do you feel connection, aliveness, tingling, or streaming sensations? Where in the body do you notice discomfort, a lack of connection, or a quality of absence or numbness? Where in the body is there a feeling of tension or stress? Contraction or expansion? Disembodiment or openness and flow? Regularly checking in with the body and mindfully gauging its state allows us to open pathways to hidden emotions, tension, and stress.

> **Emotional state.** The body is like a cup that contains the emotional waters. What's more, the body can signal us to subtle changes in our emotional experience. Sometimes the changes are subtle, while at other times they are quite strong. It is valuable to continually check in with the body and learn its varied responses

to emotional experiences. You are almost certainly familiar with the body's feelings of discomfort and uneasiness, which frequently show up as sensations in the gut. Learning to notice and be present with the subtle bodily sensations that accompany shame, sadness, fear, or anger is as important as recognizing the physical sensations that coincide with excitement, joy, and love. Sometimes there may be a feeling of numbness, and that's okay too. (Remember, in certain situations, *not feeling* is an excellent survival strategy.) There is no need to place value judgments on the signals we receive; what is important is simply to notice.

Mental state. Equally important are the signals coming from the mental self, which we can attune to simply by asking, *What is my state of mind right now?* Practice taking a witness perspective on your thinking process (i.e., *What thoughts are running in the background right now?*). Just observe. Does the mind feel busy or calm? Is it keenly focused or a bit distracted? Do your thoughts feel open and expansive or tight and constricted? Is the mind spacious or crowded? Sometimes, our thoughts flow easily with a feeling of enhanced connection, while at other times we experience tight, cyclic thought patterns. Practice observing all its states.

Relational state. How connected am I to the relational or intersubjective space—the space between us? How walled off, isolated, or withdrawn do I feel from the other person or do they feel from me? Every human emotion and experience lives in a certain relational condition. If the system is mature, open, and emergent, current experience can be held in a fluid state of relation, with warmth, connection, and curiosity. But wherever we are hurt or injured, we are unable to process our emotions in relation. (It either feels too unsafe or unwelcome, causing us to avoid or withdraw—or we might cling desperately to the other person like someone drowning and seeking rescue.)

Once we have consciously presenced the state of one system—the physical, mental, emotional, or relational—it is key to check in with the others, to notice how the state of the mind coincides with the state of the body, and so on. Practicing attunement to all four will continue to yield new discoveries in coherence.

Let's say you are in the process of making a weighty decision related to your job. As you think about what you should do, you check in with the mind and notice the presence of anxious thoughts. You might perceive these thoughts as interference, but they simply want to show themselves. Think of it like a detox process. Next, check in with your body and observe its sensations. You might have a tension in your shoulders, an ache in your lower back, or other symptoms of tensing that can signal fear and anxiety. This fear may seem related to the weighty decision you're attempting to make. Or the fear may be manifesting as a signpost that you have a limited capacity to relate with what you are experiencing.

After all, there is no wild lion stalking you for its next meal; your corporeal survival is not put at risk by your career concerns. As such, the fear or anxiety you are experiencing is not about danger but an unconscious projection of the past onto some aspect of your present— perhaps your boss, your business partner, or your imagined prospects in a given industry. And it is that projection that creates a fearful dynamic, coloring how you show up, participate, think, and behave— all of which influences how you experience life.

The unintegrated past shows up as undigested information that affects our lives today and limits our future possibility. Thus, in a real way, the past can overshadow the present, distorting our perception of the present and thereby diminishing our ability to meet it.

The more aware you become of this dynamic in your own life, the more capable you are of being present with others who are grappling with their own fears and anxieties. Developing this way allows you to provide clarifying presence, space, and time for yourself and others. Without a developed maturity in discernment, however, you will continue to participate in the unconscious dynamics played out by others and unwittingly uphold shadow or trauma agreements with them.

As we have seen, a past experience of trauma impacts our physical, emotional, and mental well-being in the present. It distorts our perception of reality, warping our experience of space and time and inhibiting our access to the present and future. The undigested past desynchronizes us, limiting our ability to connect deeply with others, to achieve flow states, or to download emergent future light. Integration is possible as we become aware of the fragmented nature of our past, bringing each of these pieces into our present awareness. This is how we integrate history.

Once again: unintegrated history is the past; integrated history is presence.

As we've explored in chapter 2 and elsewhere, resolving the past allows us to be here, now—present in the conversation. Integration brings online all ordinary functions—mental and emotional states and bodily sensations—and opens access to untapped higher, newer, more emergent capacities. It allows us to feel more deeply, sense more clearly, think more innovatively, and connect more holistically with each other, our ancestors, and our future descendants. Integration lights up structures of consciousness, illuminates ancestral wisdom, and unveils new domains in natural human intelligence. What becomes available to us are all the rich resources our species has developed over hundreds of thousands of years of human history and longer.

Integration is evolution in action.

Conversely, unintegrated history shows up as an interference, disturbance, or distortion. The fragmented past becomes today's difficult emotions, disembodiment, intractable belief systems, and dysfunctional institutions. It overshadows our experience of each other and the world. In this way, integration is not a personal endeavor I must undertake to feel better; it is my responsibility to the future of life itself. And with it comes the true innovation, fresh insights, and revelatory visions that will allow for the renewal of life on this planet.

Integration is evolution in action. It requires our participation and supports our resilience.

Here, we see the vital interplay between the individual and the collective—between one human and all humanity. As Michael Ungar, PhD, founder and director of the Resilience Research Centre at Dalhousie University, Canada, writes:

> [A]re there similarities between how a person builds and sustains psychological resilience and how a forest, community, or the business where he or she works remains successful and sustainable during periods of extreme adversity? Does psychological resilience in a human being influence the resilience of the forests (through a change in attitude toward conservation), community (through a healthy tolerance for differences), and businesses (by helping a workforce perform better) with which a person interacts? And finally, does this understanding of resilience help build better social and physical ecologies that support individual mental health, a sustainable environment, and a successful economy at the same time?[3]

Collective resilience relies on individual resilience, and vice versa. Integration is mirrored across systems. It affords us the capacity for communication and exchange, for healthy relating.

RELATIONAL INTELLIGENCE

Dr. Stephen Porges's polyvagal theory postulates that the mammalian central nervous system comes equipped with a relational plug-in. When a calm parent holds and comforts an anxious child, the nervous systems of the parent and child sync, or pair up, a bit like two Bluetooth-enabled devices. There's a synchronization happening, and it comes with a feeling like, *Ahh, that's better.* For the child, this generates a feeling of safety and allows the child to feel seen and heard and *met.*

This dimension of safety is crucial for any kind of trauma work because trauma inherently creates a lack of safety—a sense of impending threat, which is distressing and constricting. People with the developed capacity to create space to receive others are what Dr. Porges would call "trained regulators." They are skilled at helping support others in the regulation and relaxation of their own interior states, which, in turn, enhances a feeling of togetherness and belonging.

To heal the past and create greater coherence in the present—and, therefore, more availability to the future—three steps are essential: reflection, digestion, and integration.

> **Reflect.** When the nervous system is in a relaxed, regulated state, we can begin to reflect on our life and our relationships. A certain amount of inner spaciousness is needed for introspection to take place. Sometimes it comes while taking a walk, making a cup of coffee, enjoying a piece of music, or sitting by the beach and watching the waves roll in—all are activities that lend space and support relaxed reflection.

> **Digest.** When we have sufficient opportunities to reflect, we get more deeply in touch with our unintegrated experiences—all the data of life that has been shoved down into the nervous system's storage closet, including past trauma. With sufficient spaciousness and a feeling of openness, we begin to digest difficult experiences and emotions (e.g., shame, anger, despair).

> **Integrate.** The process of digestion sparks transformation. Now we can look back over our experiences and witness the whole process—from the felt sense of shutdown and numbness to activation and painful arousal. Through awareness, everything we have digested becomes integrated into our current perspective. We learn from our past, and the process expands our wisdom and understanding. Integration is the upgrading of consciousness.

Reflection promotes digestion, which nourishes and restores the nervous system. And digestion promotes integration, because now we can look at the experience with greater awareness and recognize the lessons. Integration is the incorporation of new learning and new wisdom, which expands our perspective. The part of us that is witnessing the process is becoming wiser, larger, and more inclusive. This is why, for trauma healing to occur, we need space—room for the nervous system to relax and release its frozen experiences in order to digest and integrate them.

When this process is allowed to happen, especially in the context of a supportive environment, we often experience positive changes or *posttraumatic growth*. The concept, first developed by Richard Tedeschi, PhD, and Lawrence Calhoun, PhD, in the 1990s, describes how, after experiences of adversity and trauma, many individuals experience positive transformation in various areas of life, from the quality of their relationships to deepened feelings of gratitude to a profound sense of spiritual renewal.[4] And posttraumatic growth may be a restorative process of the human nervous system.

When your nervous system is well-regulated and synchronized, you're able to participate in life, to be passionate about your work, to relate deeply and skillfully with others, and even to grow and change after traumatizing experiences.

Dr. Stephen Porges put it beautifully when he said that, as mammals, our human central nervous systems have a dual role. One is to respond to threats to our survival by activating the fight, flight, or freeze response; the other role is to engage relaxation and rest in order for digestion, reflection, self-healing, regeneration, and recuperation to occur. When your nervous system is well regulated and synchronized, you're able to participate in life, to be passionate about your work, to relate deeply and skillfully with others, and even to grow and change after traumatizing experiences. Regulation allows you to experience rest and safety and reflection. It allows you to cultivate the interior space for silence, contemplation, meditation, and presence. And it allows you to develop a sense of well-being from which you can discover greater belonging in the world around you.

Relaxation follows embodiment, and embodiment is key. It allows you to feel in touch with whatever the body is sensing. Relaxed embodiment promotes groundedness and the ability to take perspective and digest your experiences. "Digestion" in this sense is about sense-making, which is cognition plus physical sensing. If your stress level is chronically high, you are attempting to add energy/information into too little space (constricted space), which overwhelms and deregulates the nervous system. Without adequate digestion, your nervous system (much like your gut) becomes crowded and blocked. But when you feel listened to, heard, and seen, you feel comforted and can relax and digest your experiences in safety. This reveals how inner and outer coherence are companions and how they influence and are influenced by relational coherence.

It is only when you are in a state of coherence that you can provide (often in just a few minutes) a feeling of safety to a person who's highly stressed or triggered by trauma. It's less about what you say or do than it is about how you *feel* to the other person. Your regulated nervous system syncs to the other's nervous system, as if extending some of your own resources. After a while of just being together, your stressed friend might be able to slow down and take a clearer perspective on the challenging issue they're facing.

UPDATING THE YOU WITHIN ME

Let's be clear: inner/outer coherence is about more than a quality of calm or relaxation. It is also a measure of one's openness to perceiving the new or unexpected, which is why attunement asks us to stay present to what arises, not to what we expect to arise. Now, let's consider why that is so important.

When I sit across from you, my retinas take in the light around you and then transmit that data to my brain, where an image of you is formed. My ears take in the sound waves created by your voice and transmit that data to my brain. In that sense, I perceive you not entirely as you are, but as you appear within *me*. The more we interact, the more crystalized my impression of you becomes.

Generally speaking, this is a positive thing; it allows me to recognize and come to know you. But my awareness of who you are is limited by my perception, which may be distorted or reduced by my own shadow or trauma. What if you have undergone radical internal change since the last time I saw you? If I rely solely on my past perception of you, I won't notice any of your changes. A flexible, adaptable approach is vital: I must be willing to update the impression of you that is saved on my internal hard disk. That saved version of you is information about the past you, not the present you, and it is filtered through my own perception.

If I am fully present with you, the you within me gets updated, moment to moment. This is the fluid process of relating. And if at any point I stop relating to you, the you within me collapses into a facsimile of the you within me from the *past*. We can think of relating as a kind of streaming data connection that occurs in real time (and the present is the only real time).

To stay in relation, we can utilize horizontal and vertical resonance and employ the process of reflection (to become aware), digestion (to absorb, take in, or consolidate), and integration (to reorder or reorganize the past), clearing away what is no longer of use and updating the whole with new information, data, or light. After all, light is always new, always in motion. It is the flow and movement of living information. Integration, then, is the process of adding new light to the soul.

RIGHT RELATION AND DIVINE LAW

As we have seen, every lasting traumatic impact desynchronizes the body, mind, and emotions, and it fragments an aspect of life force so that it is taken offline. Symptoms of this fragmentation show up on a spectrum from rigidity to chaos, hyperactivation to numbness—an expression of restricted or reduced life flow. Integration is the process that restores these fragmented energies to the body's central channel, or flow, creating a new level of wholeness.

All things in the cosmos are possessed of wholeness, which is the natural and uninterrupted flow of consciousness, beingness, light, or life. In the mystical traditions, we refer to this condition of wholeness as *divine law,* which is mirrored in nature and provides the blueprint for everything in nature, including the healthy human nervous system. Divine law is the language of the creation of the universe, as embodied by nature. Simply put, divine law refers to natural integrity. When the law is alive in us, light (consciousness) flows throughout our bodies and minds and into the intersubjective spaces between us, illuminating our relationships and all that we do in the world. Fulfillment of divine law occurs through right relation with oneself, with others, and with the natural world. As Lao Tzu wrote,

> *All things in the cosmos are possessed of wholeness, which is the natural and uninterrupted flow of consciousness, beingness, light, or life.*

> Man follows the earth.
> Earth follows the universe.
> The universe follows the Tao.
> The Tao follows only itself.[5]

Right relation means that our words and actions are in accordance with natural integrity, which allows us to stay in relation. When our words or actions are out of alignment with life, we fall into disrelation.

Disrelation allows us to more easily hurt or lie to ourselves or other people. In other words, we have fallen out of alignment with divine law. In a state of disrelation, the flow of light within us is reduced. The stronger our transgression, the greater the internal disconnection to self and other must be.

Untended trauma narrows or blocks the passages and channels of a living system. What's more, trauma collapses potential futures. For these reasons, trauma can be understood as a violation of divine law. When the flow of light and, therefore, relation are returned, the law itself has been restored—and there is a sense of awakening, healing, and renewal.

As you can see, divine law is the ultimate expression of the power of healing relation. In the next chapter, we'll discuss a tiered process for healing and integration across the individual, ancestral, and collective levels.

8

Guidance for Facilitators of Healing

Organisms express a desire to be-in-connection, but everything
takes part in desire's yearning to become-through-mutual
transformation. Stones do. Their openness to new encounters
manifests in the slow withering of their crusts. Everything
temporal partakes in realizing desire. Everything that happens
pushes it further. The arrow of time is the arrow of desire. Time
is there because things happen, because atoms meet, because
stones breathe one another. Matter is social. Time arises because
this cosmos cannot sit still. It needs to share and connect.

—ANDREAS WEBER[1]

In order to develop normally, a child requires progressively more
complex joint activity with one or more adults who have an
irrational emotional relationship with the child. Someone's got to
be crazy about that kid. That's number one. First, last, and always.

—URIE BRONFENBRENNER

As noted in chapter 6, the term *toxic stress* (coined by researchers Andrew Garner and Michael Yogman) describes a "wide array of biological changes that occur at the molecular, cellular, and behavioral levels when there is prolonged or significant adversity in the absence of mitigating social-emotional buffers."[2] These physical brain changes are adaptive in the short term (i.e., they promote survival in a threatening environment), but they can become dysfunctional for mental or physical health over the long term. According to the science, the presence of positive social connections (i.e., "mitigating emotional buffers") is shown to lessen or even prevent the negative, long-term impacts of toxic stress. "By focusing on the safe, stable, and nurturing relationships (SSNR) that buffer adversity and build resilience," say these researchers, we are "on the cusp of a paradigm shift."[3]

This is indispensably good news. And it is the reason for this book: to outline the vital importance of human relationships, because when we show up for one another, healing change can occur—even in the midst of difficulty and accelerating change. In fact, healing integration is *only* done through a process of renewed relating, whether with another person or with the artifacts of one's past.

BEYOND TRAUMA-INFORMED CARE TO TRAUMA-INTEGRATING CARE

Everyone who works closely with patients and clients knows how important it is to be able to provide a coherent space where relating is possible. What is key here is to recognize how your own unconscious zones of unresolved past—the buried, unseen issues within you in your professional role—will invariably show up as projections onto the client (i.e., distortions of perception). In a very real way, your unaddressed shadow restricts the relational space you can provide and reduces your ability to support and assist. As a professional or a leader, your personal healing journey, alongside your dedication to transpersonal development, are critical investments in the creation of consistent, safe, nourishing, and potential-oriented work.

Put simply, walk your talk. Knowledge alone is not enough; embodied knowledge is necessary for true integrative impact.

Any time you experience an issue with a client or team member, you are seeing the edge of your own conscious universe reflected back to you. When you experience "difficulty" in the work, it is always an invitation to deepen your own integration process. Difficult clients are never "out there"; they are only "in here." Recognizing and rising to meet the needed integration creates a shift beyond trauma-informed to trauma-integrating care.

Your maturity and coherence are the instruments of healing. By utilizing the higher intelligence of relational attunement, you will be able to precisely sense where, how, and even when trauma may have occurred in the client's life, and using this instrument of attunement, you can gently support the traumatized aspects so that the individual (or group) can begin to reflect, digest, and integrate that fragmented past into the present flow of being and belonging. Your own regulated nervous system offers subtle perception of the other and acts as a kind of tuning fork, assisting the other's nervous system to regulate and cohere.

SAFE, STABLE, NURTURING RELATIONSHIPS

When you embody an open and connected energy state, you can feel it. Your energy field is "on line," and there is a fluid exchange of information between you and your environment. You feel healthier, more productive, and more engaged with life.

If you were neglected, unsupported, or frequently overpowered by your caregivers in early life, it will be more difficult for you to experience embodied states of connection and fluidity. Even as a very young child, your brain and nervous system would have learned to adapt by retracting your energies in defense of your own survival. Over time, this state of retraction will become a pattern of tension in the body. If left unaddressed, this tension will eventually make itself known through discomfort and pain—and it could prevent you from relating easily or deeply with other people—even those you love.

The good news is that the body naturally wants to let go of its tension. The only way to do so permanently, however, is to integrate the processes *behind* the tension, which were formed by the unsupportive relational context in early life. The reflexive withdrawal of energy and the tension it generates do not show up on their own; they were created *in relationship.* (Some may have even been inherited.) Thus, they cannot be integrated in isolation. You'll need to return to a relational context to do the work, but this time in a dynamic that is supportive, present, and attuned (i.e., safe, stable, and nurturing).

In the most fundamental sense, healing is simply the creation of the right container or environment: one of attunement or synchronization, which is the very language of relating.

Supportive connection is fundamentally healing and is precisely why many forms of therapy can be so beneficial for trauma survivors. Safe, stable, nurturing relationships allow a fragmented nervous system to come into co-regulation and resonance; SSNRs create space for whatever light or energy has been *absented,* so that it can be restored to the life flow as new intelligence. In the most fundamental sense, healing is simply the creation of the right container or environment: one of attunement or synchronization, which is the very language of relating.

In a conscious and resonant relational container, a developed therapist can connect with the client's interior process. There is a syncing between minds, brains, and nervous systems. This synchronization makes the subtle intersubjective field between client and therapist highly coherent and clear so that any fragmentation, disconnection, or numbness can be witnessed together.

THE EMBODIED SOUL

The soul wants to land in the body, which carries within it the wisdom of humanity's entire evolutionary story over millions of years. With healthy attachment (another way of saying "healthy relation"), the energy of the soul—our creativity and intelligence—can land well in the body. But if our relationships with caregivers and others weren't safe, supportive, and loving during the early years, we will need to contract and withhold part of ourselves from the world. This creates a chronic tension within the body-mind, which is the system attempting to stabilize itself. The price we pay down the line is that we cannot feel the flow of the river of life running through us. Instead, we often feel as if we are drowning in the experiences happening outside of us. Relational health keeps us connected to the wider river. It allows us to swim and to be swum in, gracefully.

For relational healing to occur, traditional forms of analysis and prolonged "talk therapy" are not necessarily required. The client's words about his or her past or present difficulties serve as a gateway into a deeper process. As the client shares, we can feel how and where trauma sits inside them. From there, we can begin to explore together a more refined inner awareness process, simply by witnessing the sensations that arise in the body. The client's personal story allows us to bring his or her attention to the inner world.

As integrative healers, we extend to the client a sense of safety as we gently invite them to take notice of when and where there is retraction or tension present. By tuning in with heightened presence, this energy can begin to shift. There is a feeling of release when these hidden or frozen energies are restored to the flow of the body-mind. Both the client and the therapist may experience this movement as a sudden quality of expansion or illumination, followed by a sense of settling deeper into relation.

As we discussed in chapter 3, care providers can be trained in this subtle process of attunement. As awareness and skill develop, the facilitator learns to sense into the location of trauma (or sense-locate) at the precise age or level of development that it first occurred. If the client first experienced toxic stress at age three, for example, a subtle awareness of this can be felt and recognized by the facilitator. From there, it becomes a mutual process of reflection, digestion, and integration.

For these reasons, this work must only be done with the highest expression of ethics and only after a relational container of trust and rapport is established. The practice of healing attunement is an expression of love.

Those accustomed to the preference for "clinical distance" or "clinical detachment" as a foundational norm in modern health care may be feeling some discomfort with the previous statement. Allow me to share the words of an exceptional physician, Kypros Nicolaides, MD, professor of Fetal Medicine at King's College, London, and a pioneer of the field:

> Medicine is a way of living. It's not a profession; it's not a "nine-to-five" or a "nine-to-ten" job. It's a continuous life experience. For me, this is my life. The olive tree, the building, the sharing, the trying to understand how a patient feels—being *part* of that process, not as a "detached professional" whose job is just to make a diagnosis, be polite to them, and send them off to be with their own problems.
>
> I am part of their life, at least for that short period that I am with them. I feel how they feel. I share in their happiness, and I share in their distress when things go wrong.[4]

Both love and professionalism can coexist, and it is my belief that they should, as both are needed for true healing to happen. As a healing practitioner, the only way to work sustainably and effectively is to bring to my practice my most mature self. Anything less will involve unconscious compensation, suppression, countertransference, and avoidance of closeness, which is ultimately as stressful for professionals as it is for clients. Maturity means that I am willing to feel what I experience, without needing to develop an artificial distance from my clients in order to avoid feeling touched by their pain. I must be willing to remain open and grounded—in a state of fluid relation—which is the only way to do deep, sustainable, and loving work. It is not that highly developed caregivers are never challenged by a client; it is that highly developed caregivers are willing to stay in relation through and with the experience of challenge. (In fact, there *is* no difficult client; there is only an inability or unwillingness to stay related.) For most of us, this requires real inner work.

Chapter 3 referred to the Three-Sync Practice for accessing inner/ outer, self/other synchronization, and it's useful to return to as we seek to understand relationality. Creating safety and a refined sense of attunement allows the client to notice when there is a sense of separation (a feeling that we are no longer in fluid connection, as if the "phone line" is breaking up). Simply by noticing that separating quality with care, it can often be dissolved and a feeling of fluid relation restored. Remember, the body communicates directly with the body; emotions resonate with emotions; and mind understands mind. We don't need a mental translation of emotional content.

Attunement can be used to enhance and deepen our virtual interactions as well, such as during Zoom calls, when writing texts and emails, and during virtual therapy sessions. When practiced, attunement makes the virtual space feel warmer and more authentic and assists us in creating more precise relation and, therefore, a more supportive relational container. This container is the birthing ground of posttraumatic growth and the foundation for resilience and flourishing. In this space, the light of awareness is restored to the system, and the life force brightens and expands, producing new states of aliveness, curiosity, and insight. Establishing this environment through precise attunement is initially a complex and sophisticated process, but it is also the simplest, most natural expression of healthy relating.

HEIDI WOHLHÜTER ON LISTENING
TO THE "UNHEARD PLACES"

Heidi Wohlhüter is a behavioral therapist and supervisor for therapists, teams, and psychologists, supporting them in their shadow work and professionalization.

What I've learned through my work is a way of seeing, in which I learn to see with all of my capacity to perceive—with all of my feeling senses, with all of my bodily perceptions and sensations. With this approach, I'm not only listening to what my clients say with words, I'm also listening through the nervous-system connection. And this allows me to attune to *more* than just their words, but also to a deeper place within them. It's as if there's a kind of atmosphere of information and feeling that surfaces.

For example, I might be listening to a client in this way and suddenly experience a chemical taste in my mouth. When I mention this to him, he might tell me that when he was a child, his mother was undergoing strong chemical treatments for cancer. I happen to know from my own life how my husband smelled when he was undergoing cancer treatment, but just imagine what this meant for this client as a little boy! I didn't know that this connection existed until I told him about the chemical taste I was experiencing. I just named it and then he made the association to his mother's cancer. This is a very different way to enter my client's world, to be present with his experiences.

Another example is the way this kind of listening and perceiving allows me to experience with my clients their dissociated states. For me, this is a very new aspect of healing— learning to be present with a client in the place where she is suffering, where it's dark, where she was originally alone, and no one was there. It's a kind of miracle that we can go back there together now. And when we do, something often changes or shifts; something new is experienced.

When a client allows me to enter with them into a time or place where they felt lost in the dark, and I can describe what I perceive and how I feel there, they are suddenly no longer alone. It's like, *"Wow, there's someone who sees me. There's someone who feels me."* This moment creates a new reference for connection. And maybe this is where healing starts for them. I don't want to speak in generalities, but in this example, this is where healing starts.

In psychiatric training, a therapist learns the symptoms, the "criteria," for when a client has dissociated so that they can then tell the client to come back into the body. But this approach isn't always what is helpful. It may be more appropriate just to respect and acknowledge the act of disassociation, and even to explore how dissociation was felt as the best option. As we do this, a new movement appears. Of course, for most who work in a clinical setting and who may see many clients per week, this can be difficult to do—to enter these feeling states with our clients. But when we can do this kind of deeper work with them, there is often a healing effect.

The more space I have available in me for the person who is sitting in front of me, the more information and clarity about them I receive. There's something very subtle but very real happening, where my openness and attunement allow me to help make the invisible visible. It isn't something that *I* do; it's something I am in service to. And I feel deeply privileged to do this work with people.

MULTISYSTEMS INTEGRATION

The individual and the collective, the atom and the field, are an interdependent whole. No matter how isolated someone feels, no one exists entirely outside of or apart from their family, ancestry, community, or culture. Fitting our interdependent systems back together in fluid and "right relationship" to one another is perhaps the highest and most vital aim of the healing endeavor.

Our willingness to more fully embrace human interrelation and interdependence will ultimately change how we engage in health and healing across all domains, including science, medicine, and psychotherapy. The inseparability of persons is the foundation of the three broad categories or modalities of healing that I utilize in my work (we'll be exploring two of these further in chapters 9 and 10). They are:

- the Individual Trauma Integration Process (ITIP)
- the Ancestral Trauma Integration Process (ATIP)
- the Collective Trauma Integration Process (CTIP)[5]

It is vital to understand that all three modalities are equally essential for any true and lasting healing to occur. Certainly, individuals can and do experience many types of personal healing in their lives, even when their families or societies are unwilling or unable to do the same. Still, deeper layers of systemic healing work can and must be done. The beauty is that once we begin multisystems healing work at any level—the personal, ancestral, or collective—there is a kind of retrocausal shift: more light, clarity, and possibility become available in the vertical, horizontal, ancestral, or social fields. And when that happens, we can *feel* it.

In my work I use the term *IAC fluidity* to describe the "liquification" of trauma across all three dimensions or scales—the individual (I), the ancestral (A), and the collective (C). We say that trauma freezes, disconnects, makes stagnant, or absences an aspect of the self and stores it away in the shadow until it can be safely processed. Individual, ancestral, or collective fluidity is, therefore, the return and re-presencing of shadow back into the larger flow or process of light/life.

Of course, in practice, this work also requires competence and refined ethics. We must exhibit maturity, integrity, and balanced sensitivity, and we must inhabit an awareness of whole-systems healing by starting with ourselves. We, and the healing professions we represent, must become both trauma informed and trauma integrating.

Each of the three primary modalities of healing—ITIP, ATIP, and CTIP—is:

- relational

- integrational

- presence based

- response based

- established through subtle attunement

- grounded in human interdependence

- capacity generating

- fluid

- emergent

To heal repetitive, disrelational, distant, and absenced relationships, we must strive for emergent, creative, relational, warm, and connected processes.

The **Individual Trauma Integration Process (ITIP)** looks at an individual's biographical trauma—from unresolved injuries rooted in early attachment to the presence of severe one-time or ongoing adversity. To take a more complete view, ITIP is concerned with the client's family system, as well as with any traumatizing aspects of their social or cultural conditioning. We undertake ITIP through the relational container described above.

In the wise words of Dr. Gabor Maté in the film *The Wisdom of Trauma*, "Children don't get traumatized because they're hurt. They get traumatized because they're alone with their hurt."[6] As healers, we provide a felt sense of safety for our clients by feeling *with* them (but not *as* them). Through grounded, empathetic attunement, we can extend some of the resilience within our own nervous systems to help them regulate their own. Where there was once absence, we bring grounded presence. Where there was isolation, we offer a feeling of togetherness. The client's nervous system should receive our attention without feeling pushed or pressured or left alone. This creates an open channel—an "extended mind," if you will—so that as the client recounts their experiences, we can perceive more clearly the architectures of trauma that reside within them and offer more precise support. This is an unspoken but deeply harmonic process.

If the client experienced shock as a two year old, for example, the therapist needs to match the energetic environment that *was needed* by the client at that stage of life, which is always about safer, more stable, and nurturing connections.

Remember, trauma is the disorganized part within an organism or system, which then transfers that disorganization (or incoherence) onto its environment. If there is unmet trauma within the therapist, their own fragmentation will prevent precise attunement and can be felt as a sensation of pressure on the process. For this reason, it is vitally important for any healing professional to get in touch with their own disorganization (trauma) before it can disrupt the therapeutic process. As facilitators of healing, we must commit to ongoing healing work for ourselves, including regular contemplative practices, such as the Three-Sync Practice (attuning to the body and noticing any areas that are open or tight, energized or numb, stressed or resonant).

Relating is, after all, a process whereby *I arise in you, as you arise in me.* If I am not working to integrate what is disorganized within me, I may unconsciously project it onto you. And because of the nature of the client/therapist relationship, the client is more likely to take in my unconscious projections in the form of harmful introjections (i.e., the unconscious internalization of the other's voice or ideas, especially where the other is perceived as an authority or authoritative figure). To engage in healing work, we must heal, not harm.

The good news is that as we heal ourselves, we make healing more possible for others. To get in touch with what needs healing, we can connect through the body, which is a sculptural story of our lives. To get in touch with the interior, one can connect through the exterior, and vice versa. The mind and body are designed to radiate with embodied light. We are all meant to feel our own life force, to see through illumined eyes, to know ourselves as purposeful and alive.

The **Ancestral Trauma Integration Process (ATIP)** is concerned with the unintegrated injuries within a person's family, including their family of ancestors. An effective use of ATIP teaches practitioners to sense into and discern the presence of family members and/or past ancestors whose unresolved traumas have been passed down to the client, who still carries them today. Additionally, ATIP seeks to understand the epigenetic story, as well as the emotional and environmental habits that inform the client's mind and body and that may be reflected in the systemic challenges they face.

Note: there is a vital difference between *imagining* a client's ancestors and fundamentally *sensing* the information their ancestors bring forward. You might have some intellectual knowledge or even just an imagined version of the ancestors, but what you really need can only be found with intentional attunement, simply by noticing what arises in the body, the mind, or the emotions as you think about and tune in with the ancestors. When you tune in to your own great-grandmother, for example, what do you notice in your body or emotions? What inner images or thoughts do you experience? Once you tune into the first feeling, sensation, or image that arises, you are then given access to other deeply stored information. Still, even if the only feeling you can perceive is numbness or absence, that is precisely the information you need to work with. Multigenerational healing is about restoring the ancestral narrative—physically, emotionally, mentally, and spiritually.

Each of us represents millions of years of evolutionary intelligence. Like Russian dolls, we are not just the bodies and personalities other people perceive on the surface; we are each an exquisite amalgam of everything that came before and much that is new and particular or unique to us.

In a very real way, you *are* your ancestors. Yet, at the time of this writing, the idea that we can engage in ancestral healing is still very much at the margins of what is accepted as possible. Very soon, however, I believe many people will accept the concept of ancestral healing as self-evident. Even now, contemporary psychology is slowly beginning to take more seriously the validity of therapeutic techniques such as Family Constellation Therapy or Systemic Constellation Therapy. Its founder, Bert Hellinger, was influenced in part by the work of Ivan Boszormenyi-Nagy, the late Hungarian-American psychiatrist who helped found the field of family therapy. Boszormenyi-Nagy took a comprehensive approach by seeking to understand the many dimensions of experience and development that play a role in human life—a spectrum that includes the individual, interpersonal, existential, systemic, and intergenerational influences that inform and impact who we are and how we show up.

Each of us represents millions of years of evolutionary intelligence.

With this complex and multidimensional family systems view, Boszormenyi-Nagy proposed four domains of "relational reality" that influence us. These four domains are:

1. Facts (e.g., bodily health, genetic influences, social background, socioeconomic status, and biographic details)

2. Individual psychology

3. Systemic transactions (e.g., social rules, power, alignments, feedback, etc.)

4. Relational ethics.[7]

Family and systems therapy has something else in common with the approach I describe: the recognition that severe adversity continues to impact survivors and their descendants, sometimes long after the initial trauma or the original survivors have passed.

Here is the miracle: When you engage in ancestral healing, you will know that it has been effective when you begin to see practical, tangible results in your life. You may start to notice interesting shifts in those around you. A parent who has been struggling with aging and independence may become more at peace with this essential, rite-of-life passage. A previously estranged sibling may get back in touch. A child or grandchild may start to exhibit radical, forward leaps in emotional and psychological development. And you will feel similar shifts of your own.

By restoring the shards of the past, we bring renewal to our lives in this moment, today, now.

I have seen many family systems change through individual and ancestral trauma work. Estranged family members suddenly reconnect and relationships begin to heal, with family members suddenly demonstrating a desire to do real inner work. When we bring light into places of systemic stagnation and familial absence that were created by trauma, a whole new order of fresh energy begins to shift and move—and that new movement results in healing change that is often very surprising.

As you can see, ancestral healing isn't something we do for the dead, per se; it is the conscious act of returning to the living of a true birthright. By restoring the shards of the past, we bring renewal to our lives in this moment, today, now. It is *this* that makes it possible for future descendants to enter a better world: one with more hope, more light, more possibility.

By utilizing the openness of the subtle energetic nervous system, we can attune to the client and sense-locate their ancestors within our own bodies and nervous systems (see chapter 10). From here, we begin to notice any points of trauma that have been inherited. Again, this process doesn't require that the client share their family narrative. In fact, unless the client prefers to, discussion about the past isn't important. It is merely a process of attunement and mutually sensing what is present or absent.

In this model, the therapist's objective is simply to sense into and access the point of trauma in the client and then to help guide or assist them in getting in touch with the information that is stored in their own system (more about this in chapter 9). We are helping to revive any frozen and dissociated aspects that were split off at the place and time of the trauma—whether it happened to them or to their forebears— and from there, we help these fragmented parts to become integrated.

Ancestral traumas of all kinds can create attachment injuries for future generations. It is vital that any facilitator of ancestral healing begins with the integration of their own family wounds. To hold someone else's ancestral pain, we must learn to hold—to reflect on, digest, and integrate—our own.

By training to attune to the vertical or ancestral field, we can learn to sense-locate information about the client's parents and other generations. With presence, resonance, and an open mental frame, we can uncover quite a lot about the ancestral line, in fact. No matter what we find in the process, however, simply "looking at" or describing the information is not enough to unlock and restore these fragments. We must witness what is in need of restoration, *feel* what is present, and allow it to move through us. In chapter 9, we discuss ancestral healing in more detail.

The **Collective Trauma Integration Process (CTIP)** brings communities or groups of people together with the purpose of sensing into and integrating their hidden cultural and historic wounds. Collective traumas may include injuries left behind in the wake of violence, deprivation, slavery, war, occupation/colonialization, genocide, and any other human-caused trauma. Using the CTIP allows us to witness the deep scars that continue to shape our societies, often without our knowledge or notice. (CTIP is discussed in further detail in chapter

10, and a process for CTIP is described in my 2020 book, *Healing Collective Trauma.*)

We are all aware of communities that are surrounded by a heavy trauma matrix or shadow landscape. In these places, it is common to observe broken families and dysfunctional schools, churches, hospitals, and other fractured social structures. There may be a visible underground economy, heightened crime, and economic despair. It is as if trauma were the secret architect of the community itself.

If you were to visit a region or neighborhood like this, you might notice around you a heavy feeling in the air. At some point, communal trauma resulted in the "endarkenment" of the landscape so that depression, addiction, discord, and human suffering remain present just under the surface—or right out in the open. You don't have to be a sociologist or even a mystic to detect its presence; you can simply feel it. No one would argue that the darkness or heaviness isn't there.

There are many things we can do to help heal the suffering in our communities, but to begin liberating ourselves from the burden of systemic trauma requires a multisystems approach. After all, community pain is also, by nature, the pain of families and individual people.

The degree of past trauma that is carried by our societies today appears to have a direct impact on the whole of the natural world. Ecosystem collapse is the culminating manifestation of untended cultural suffering and the disrelation or separation it promotes. Scientists recognize that trauma can arrest human development, and it is clear that collective trauma can obstruct societal development. What is less understood are the ways that repeated, unresolved systemic trauma can catalyze the downfall of civilizations.

In a very real way, by choosing to process the wounds of the past together, through subtle attunement to the individual, ancestral, and collective fields, we may discover not only how to prevent or even reverse impending collapse, but how to spark the creation of a whole-systems upgrade, a whole new Earth.

PROCESS-ORIENTED WORK

In the 1970s, Jungian analyst and author Arnold Mindell founded pro-cess-oriented psychology, or Process Work. The development of Process Work was influenced by Mindell's training in applied physics at MIT and ETH Zürich, as well as his studies in Taoism and shamanism. He recognized that the unconscious mind reveals itself both symbolically and phenomenologically; the unconscious is expressed physically in our bodies, materially in our relationships, and visually in our dreams.

Mindell used the term *process* to refer to "changes in perception, to the variation of signals experienced by an observer."[8] Process Work involves observational, theoretical, and practical techniques that have as much application for individuals as they do for large-scale groups. "The various aspects of personal life," writes Mindell, "which psy-chology has referred to until now as dreams, body life, relationship conflicts, and illness, can be reevaluated in terms of sensory-oriented channels such as proprioception, kinesthesis, visualizations, auditions, and compositions of these channels." The essence of Process Work is determining the pattern *behind* the process. A process worker "lis-tens to the verbs people use, watches their body motions, notices his own reactions, discovers those he tends to neglect . . ." Like Taoism, Process Work is all about noticing the process itself and observing the river's flow.

The capacity to witness one's process is a skill set that requires practice, especially in observing the psyche's own defense mechanisms against the process. Our automatic, unconscious motivations and behaviors are by their nature hidden to us, so it is the duty of any ear-nest process worker to illuminate the dark. The aim is to always make an ally of the defense rather than to unconsciously collude with it.

As therapists, healers, or facilitators, it is our job to become prac-ticed at witnessing our own process, as well as another's, and, indeed, to witness self and other (or self *in* other/other *in* self) in tandem. This mutual presencing practice undergirds my work with individuals and groups, and it is key to integrative healing.

Let's consider what this process might look like. As you work with a client, you might take a kind of internal x-ray of the client's body so that when he talks about his fear, you can notice how that fear shows itself inside him. For example, you might observe that the client controls his fear by pulling his energy out of the legs and centralizing it in the lower abdomen. Refining perception and attunement brings forward these observations, which are communicated as reflections, not as diagnoses or absolute truths.

When you ask him to notice the sensations of his body, the client might even say, "I feel like there's a stone in my belly." And you can sense this stonelike sensation along with him, receiving input from him to verify your observations.

"Do you suppose you have been using that stone since childhood as a way of controlling your fear?" you might ask. You can only do this with your client—feel the stone of his fear in the abdomen and sense how long it has been a habit—if you are sitting with awareness in your own body, noticing the sensation in your own legs, your own belly. When you and your client are sitting *in relation*, you are fully attuned, and your body becomes a reference guide to your client's process.

Now, if I am sitting across from you but not *with* you, I will not be able to feel your process. Perhaps I am only five or six feet away physically, but it will feel as though we are at a greater distance. In this scenario, to know anything at all about what is happening for you, I will have to rely on what you tell me about it; I will not simply feel it with you.

Let's say that I am with a client who has shut down or absented her fear. I may gently ask whether it is possible for her to tell me what she feels, to which she may respond, "I don't feel anything." She is numb.

"Ahh, good," I might say. "Let's stay with the possibility that not feeling is better than feeling." (The idea is not to *change* the process, but to be with it.) Not feeling anything, including one's overwhelming fear, is sometimes the most intelligent response.

Simply by becoming conscious of the absence she feels, the client will begin to synchronize herself with the numbness—and as this happens, the numbness will *start to shift*. The simple act of witnessing her numbness to fear may even catalyze a profound release of sadness. This is a natural and beautiful part of the change process, because now she can feel the fear that had previously been hidden.

From here, I might ask the client, "When you feel into this fear, what happens to our connection?" Unsurprisingly, when she feels her fear, she is less able to feel connected. Fear closes the connection so that there is the impression of greater distance between us—greater separation.

"Now, see if you can feel your fear *and* the distance," I might say. Doing this illuminates the feeling of separation with consciousness. "Now let's feel it together, the fear and the distance," I might say. "Let's just stay here with this."

The process of "going numb" might have been stuck in a time loop, possibly repeating over decades. But in a moment of embodied awareness, there is a new feeling of safety, which allows us to release the habit of numbness. In its place, the nervous system can more fully touch the present moment.

Again, we are not trying to change anything for the client; we are simply guiding them to notice and honor their defenses with shared presence and attention. There is no pathologizing in this dance; there is nothing a person "should" or "shouldn't" feel. There is only that which is arising; there is only the river.

In her stunning book, *Poet Warrior*, Joy Harjo, United States Poet Laureate, musician, playwright, and author, writes:

> We are all here to serve each other. At some point we have to understand that we do not need to carry a story that is unbearable. We can observe the story, which is mental; feel the story, which is physical; let the story go, which is emotional; then forgive the story, which is spiritual, after which we use the materials of it to build a house of knowledge.[9]

Everything we learn about life's process by witnessing and feeling it together becomes beam and stone and mortar: the tools we need to create a house of shared human wisdom.

EMBODIED FACILITATION

It is a strange but certain fact that the strategies we utilize to adapt to and survive our traumas are the very same that, when prolonged and habituated, prevent us from flourishing. Over time, these same noble defenses, the automatic and unconscious mechanisms employed by our evolutionary nervous system, may even result in our destruction. It is key, then, that we become aware of our defense patterns and that we acknowledge and befriend them. After all, the survival strategies we choose have a great deal to teach us.

This work is equally as necessary for therapists and facilitators of healing as it is for those who seek guidance on the path to healing. In the supervisions I conduct for the therapists who work with me, we are always on the lookout for new or old defense patterns. We keep an eye on what is happening inside us in response to our clients' processes, and we spend time sharing and working through those reactions together.

A common defense strategy we may notice in ourselves and our clients is that of over-mentalization. This is a top-down defense that prioritizes cognition over sensation. We would do well to remember that cognition is not always the same as insight; just because we think it, does not make it true or right or total.

When over-mentalization shows up, I am more likely to identify with my mental ideas and images, even when they are out of alignment with my body's sensations and perceptions. Thinking about you is not the same as sensing you; by prioritizing my mentalizations about you, I lose my connection to you. And wherever relation is broken, a great deal of wisdom is lost.

Behind the defense of over-mentalization, it is as if I am watching a prerecorded video of you. All the data I can experience about you is limited to the scripted, unchanging version of you that I create with my mind. If we are in fluid relation, however, I will experience you as a kind of live stream. My body's full spectrum of awareness is available to know and experience you, not just the mind. This relational live stream is more interactive; new and emergent information can come through.

As therapists and facilitators of healing, it is our responsibility to stay in live-stream mode. And it is our duty to notice and course-correct when the relational function between ourselves and our clients has collapsed. Again, being in process is about honoring whatever is real and present in the moment. We must be keenly aware that all defense patterns are an intelligent function of the nervous system and that a client's particular defenses have developed because they needed them in difficult times. The object is not to get rid of the defense—attempting that would be a mistake—but simply to bring awareness to it. For example, if a client is asked how he feels about something and responds that he doesn't feel anything, the integrative intervention is never about getting him to feel but simply about making the process of numbing or absencing his feelings a conscious one. Once the client is aware of the numbing as a defense, his nervous system can open and expand, and he can make the choice to feel when the circumstances are right.

By making the defense an ally, we can more creatively collaborate in the healing process. However, if my client's defense mechanism somehow triggers or exhausts me, I need to recognize that my own inner wounds and shadows have been activated in such a way that I no longer have the space to offer my client for supportive healing.

The key to integrative Process Work is to stay as present to our own reactions as we strive to be with the clients or groups with whom we work. When a client is sharing with us, when and where do we fall out of relation? If we fail to stay in the flow and to observe our own internal defenses, we remain unconscious—and very little healing work gets done. The more unconscious we are, the lower the vibration and the more fog there is clouding the intersubjective space. Frequently, we accept this fog and the built-in feeling of distance that it generates as normal; however, it is anything but. If we assign *normal* to mean "healthy," we can agree it is far healthier to clear the fog and more accurately sense, see, and feel one another. This is the skill set of the embodied therapist.

Another common defense strategy we see in the relational exchange is less commonly discussed. It occurs when we respond to feelings of overwhelm by flattening or collapsing our awareness of the other person back into a two-dimensional image or impression. This regression of awareness from three-dimensional into simple two-dimensional is not just happening in our thoughts about the other person. It coincides with our own disembodiment.

As I collapse my awareness of you, some part of my own body must be absent from my awareness. By shutting down the body's sense perceptions, I collapse my felt experience of you into a 2D representation. In essence, you become a poster, not a person. I do this to avoid pain or overwhelm. I can no longer sense you in me; I feel separate from you and look only at the poster I have made of you. If I cannot sense you within me, it's possible for me to cause you harm. (As long as I can sense you within me and myself within you, I can never hurt you; it would be like harming myself.) As we all know, hurting people hurt people.

A poster is merely a mental image and is unconnected through the body to nature. In the collapse of awareness to 2D, we can no longer feel our proximity to natural laws or the organizing principle behind all things. In 3D, we are identified with the body. We can think of 2D collapses as flattened, disembodied energies that are just hanging around in the unconscious, like logjams blocking the flow of the river of life. For that flow to return, the collapsed energies must be reembodied and integrated. Trauma leaves behind these 2D facsimiles or ghosts, which long to be integrated.

MARKUS HIRZIG ON ATTUNING TO THE
SUBTLE FIELD IN CLIENT WORK

Markus Hirzig, a trained physiotherapist, is a core member of the Assistant Team for the Academy of Inner Science and has worked with Thomas Hübl since 2002.

When a client comes to see me, I listen as they talk about their symptoms. And as they are talking, their words will naturally begin to highlight the structure of their energetic background. As they talk, this structure—the substance of their physical body and their energetic body—"lights up."

As I sense this happening, I just gently hold that connection because many of us have never experienced that connection on many levels. Instead, we are used to being approached in a physical way but, shall we say, in a relatively *empty* physical way. So, when someone is "touched" physically or energetically through simple connection, there is a distinct difference when the connection comes from someone who is embodied. The connection feels full.

When a person is more disconnected from the physical experience, however—perhaps coming from a more mental approach—then the connection feels empty. And that changes the atmosphere of the space we are talking in, the intersubjective space.

The first [quality that is needed for this work] is simply to be interested in and deeply curious about the integrative approach. From the perspective of realism or positivism, the subtle experiences we are describing here are viewed as nonsense. So, there must be an interest and an openness. To "touch" people and be touched through this subtle field of perception, we must be willing to establish our connection at this frequency, shall we say, where every physiological or material sense—seeing, feeling, hearing—also has a subtle energetic component. There must be an interest in training those interior, intersubjective sensory capacities.

Doing so changes the atmosphere we are sitting in, so that it feels fuller and richer. The space between us [or the shared space *within* us] can begin to feel so full that it connects us. There is no longer a feeling of separation, but one of relatedness, togetherness. When more deeply attuned to, we see that the intersubjective space between us is overflowing with information and connection. . . . There is a sense of shared exchange—a subtle connection that imparts a great deal of information.

[For example,] sometimes when you're working with a client, there is this sense as if another person has entered the room. The presence of this other person may just be a kind of knowing, like, "Oh, this is the mother." Or "This is the father."

When this happens, I will simply ask my client, "When I bring up your father, what occurs to you?"

Now, when I say this, I am not necessarily asking about the real person who is the client's father but more about their relationship, especially the still unintegrated parts of their connection. I might ask the client to share what really worked well between them and also what didn't. It doesn't matter whether the client's father is dead or living. Either way, any unresolved aspects of their relationship still exist within the client, and this is what we work with together. I have observed again and again how when we can connect with these other persons or other presences, the client's healing process moves along faster and tends to go much deeper.

Even if the therapist or facilitator doesn't connect to these other energies [or ancestral presences], it might be helpful simply to hold the qualities of the connection in the moment—to hold the client and the relationship with the mother in awareness together. Notice what's flowing and what's not flowing; what's open and what's not open.

Something like that sounds a little bit—or maybe very—esoteric. And it might be, *but it works.*

PROCESS WORK AND IAC-FLUIDITY METHODOLOGIES

Methods or techniques speak to the practices and skills we utilize in any given approach to human life care. Acquiring knowledge and mastery in demonstrably competent modes of healing is, of course, vitally important and should be the ethical standard of approach. Still, the idea of "methods" can unintentionally solidify a living process into a static form. Relying on a firm method may lead us to believe we already know *how* to heal and may limit what we can learn through a more fluid approach.

Developing IAC fluidity (Individual Ancestral Collective fluidity) is like learning to play jazz; it happens as we do it. We are working in and with the unfolding process of healing rather than being fixated on applying exact methods or techniques to make something work. When beneficial techniques or exercises show up as part of the unfolding (i.e., as a product of emergent healing and conscious relation), we can trust that those exercises are the right thing to do in the moment.

Facilitating trauma work takes a high degree of skill, psychological and ethical maturity, and transpersonal awareness. Successful facilitators will also possess a depth of knowledge and training on trauma, but more important than cognitive expertise is the facilitator's degree of openness and fluidity. Trauma integration work—whether with individuals, a community of ancestors, or large groups of unrelated persons—is a lesson in *staying in the flow of relation* through mutual awareness, presence, and embodiment.

When the inner world and outer world are integrated and in sync, the facilitator is reading the book of life directly. It is a moment-to-moment process of fluid relation, and all the information the facilitator needs to be supportive is available in the streaming connection. When a facilitator is out of sync and, therefore, in separation rather than in fluid relation, they won't be able to perceive accurately, or they won't be able to trust what they receive.

As facilitators, we are only able to accurately perceive the client or the group's process to the degree that we are present and open to our own. Presence itself is the portal through which a higher order of energy and information can be downloaded. The deeper and more skillful one's presence, the more effective the portal and the deeper the healing potential.

We might say that a good facilitator is someone who is fully "online." No matter what surfaces through the relational work, the facilitator can stay attuned, present, and awake to their own and the client's inner process. They demonstrate inner and outer coherence, offer co-regulatory capacities, and can deeply listen and carefully transmit the vital yet exquisitely subtle information that arises in the relational field.

In her stunning memoir, Joy Harjo, American Poet Laureate and author, writes of the wisdom that can be gained and must be nurtured. "My great-grandfather reminds me that we need to keep within the long-rooted mind," she writes. "Because of the longer roots, we have a larger structure of knowing from which to take on understanding."[10] These are the tools we use to "build our house of knowledge" so that we may continue to grow and evolve together, with our planet, and among the greater cosmic community of worlds.

Even our darkest shadow is potential light, waiting to be actualized and to offer new solutions, new possibilities, and new growth. That light needs a living person with a body and its chi to make it into the world. However shaded or fragmented we may be, a thriving, integrated world is waiting to become.

9

Ancestral Healing

We're all ghosts. We all carry, inside us,
people who came before us.
—LIAM CALLANAN

I salute the light within your eyes where the whole Universe
dwells. For when you are at that center within you and
I am at that place within me, we shall be one.
—CRAZY HORSE, OGLALA LAKOTA SIOUX (1877)

n the contemporary West, we have, by and large, developed cultures that no longer offer either reverence or remembrance of the ancestors. Although there are religious groups such as the Roman Catholic Church and the Eastern Orthodox Church that continue to observe rites that venerate the dead—in particular, those persons regarded as saints, who are believed to serve as intercessors between the living faithful and God—the numbers and practices have notably lessened compared to other cultures and times. Whether or not we acknowledge our familial or other lineages, however, honoring the ancestors serves an important unifying and restorative communal function.

But for the deep roots of our respective genealogical tree, its branches would never have leafed or flowered and resulted in you or me. No matter who we are, the roots of those trees bind us together, stretching back further than the imagination can follow to our common ancestors in time. Those roots reach back to the emergence of humankind and even further: to the arrival of Earth's earliest life-forms, and then still further to the birth and death of stars. It is perhaps wise to think of humanity's roots as living data cables, which channel the light, energy, and information of life. This vibrant, ancient pathway transcends time and is a vital resource for the living. Through our ancestors, we ground ourselves in and as the planet.

When a person feels especially disconnected from their family of ancestors, an essential energy resource gets cut, as if they are suddenly unplugged. This has real effects. At one end of the continuum, the person may struggle with a general lack of energy, motivation, or purpose in their lives. At the other end, they may experience heightened stress, a drive to overwork, the urgent appetite for achievement, or the pressing desire for status and other forms of external validation and recognition. Frequently, the lack of ancestral resourcing results in a quality of rootlessness, disembodiment, and/or an unstable sense of personal, cultural, or social identity. The common injury among all these symptoms is the critical absence of belonging—the lack of a sense of home and place and community.

Yet the world's ancient wisdom traditions, including its many rich indigenous cultures, understood the importance of human ancestors. One does not come to exist without them and cannot continue to exist well without connection to them. This vital truth has largely been lost on contemporary societies, despite our many technological advancements in genealogical research and genetic testing.

In the wise words of Senegalese poet Birago Diop, "The dead are not dead."[1] Whether we feel bonded to our forebears or woefully detached, the ancestors live on inside us—in our bodies, brains, habits, preferences, reactions, and other patterns of feeling, thought, and behavior.

In fact, our biological nervous system is rooted in and wired from the greater collective nervous system, which is not bound to linear time or to any given place. Our ancestors did not and do not exist "somewhere else," separated from us by continent or calendar. They are not *behind* us but within us.

In *Ancestral Medicine,* author Daniel Foor, PhD, observes:

> Like Russian nesting dolls, our experience of recent family ancestors rests within larger patterns of lineage, culture, and human prehistory. Our oldest ancestors lived in Africa at least two hundred thousand years ago. In this way, the ancestors express the collective wisdom of humanity. They are elders who remember our full evolutionary journey as human beings, and they are custodians of our genetic and cultural memory.[2]

Each of us belongs to a great lineage of beings that stretches forever back into the recesses of unrecorded time and forever forward into the future. No one stands alone in the great scheme or the great web.

In this context, we can see that "ancestral trauma" is simply another way of saying familial or interpersonal disrelation. Healthy, integrated ancestries become pathways of wisdom and intelligence for living families and communities. They bridge emotional and social capacities by supporting our connection to others and to the earth itself. A healthy and vibrant relationship to the ancestors

Each of us belongs to a great lineage of beings that stretches forever back into the recesses of unrecorded time and forever forward into the future.

locates us more wholly in the here and now. With this in mind, let's look at some of the common consequences and invisible manifestations of unmetabolized ancestral trauma.

If you want to see how trauma shows up in your family, start a family business. Novels, plays, films, and hit television series relish the drama of a family in conflict or crisis. Consider the real-world legacy empires that collapse from infighting, competition, and greed between siblings or relatives. In the evergreen narrative of the broken family, it is easy to see how the "sins of the father" cause no end of trouble for his children and their children. Even when real examples of families torn asunder hit the headlines, it can appear as if their conflicts are all about the business or the crime or the splashy public disagreement. But look beneath the petty sibling rivalry, personality clashes, and professional disagreements and you are likely to discover a family system riddled with the unconscious fear of scarcity, sourced in the preexisting condition known as *trauma*.

Trauma produces a sense of lack—a feeling of "not enough." Not enough time or money or other vital resources to go around. Not enough support or recognition or value. Not enough health or life or safety. Worst of all, not enough love.

Whether dealing with an embattled family business, a toxic war over inheritance, a family torn apart by unacknowledged abuse or neglect, or an estranged, distant, and unattached family that no longer speaks, the surface symptoms of familial disrelation always represent something far deeper—something a broken family's ancestors likely generated or suffered in many of the very same ways.

An important note: not everyone has been raised by their genetic relations, of course. Integration work with an individual's lineage of caregivers, whether they are blood relatives or not, is often just as important to the healing process as work done with genetic relations. For simplicity's sake, I will primarily use terms that describe bloodlines, but keep in mind that "milk lines" are also important and should be included.

THE ANCESTRAL NERVOUS SYSTEM

We have discussed in previous chapters the fact that most people acknowledge only the nervous system's gross physical structures, including the brain, and that they believe that each person's central nervous system is individual, separate, and distinct. Yet, from a deeper perspective, there is also a collective nervous system, which includes the ancestral nervous system and constitutes the subtler aspect of an extended system that encodes the ancestral experiences—the information vital to our function, but which preceded our lives. This broader system surpasses temporal and spatial boundaries, and it serves as a kind of Ethernet link, not just to the biological or genetic conditions of our forebears, but to the accumulated memories, skills, talents, strengths, and wisdom our predecessors generated in the course of their lives.

I have described how, as therapists, facilitators, and healers, we can learn to sense and attune to the nervous systems of individual clients in the course of healing work with them. Likewise, we can learn to sense and attune to a client's system of ancestral relations. Often, an especially attuned therapist will begin to feel or sense a client's ancestors even before the aim of ancestral healing arises. All shamanic and many Eastern traditions have long understood this work as essential to healing; however, a renewed awareness of the subtle presence of ancestors is beginning to emerge for many other practitioners.

To undertake any form of ancestral integration work in earnest, some cognitive understanding is of course necessary. It is much more important, however, that we learn to *feel into* our own ancestors. How does your connection to your parents, grandparents, or great-grandparents feel? Can you sense a ready connection, or is there a quality of distance or absence? There are no wrong answers. Whatever you discover as you undertake such an exercise is precisely the information that you then need to work with.

Just as your parents and their parents passed down to you many physical and likely behavioral traits (e.g., coarse dark hair; an easygoing disposition; or a talent for music), you also inherited their unresolved struggles. Like unpaid taxes, any portion of an ancestor's past that was left undigested is conveyed to their descendants. Your forebears' unmetabolized energies live within you today, and frequently the repetitions or retraumatizations you experience in your lifetime are as much theirs as your own.

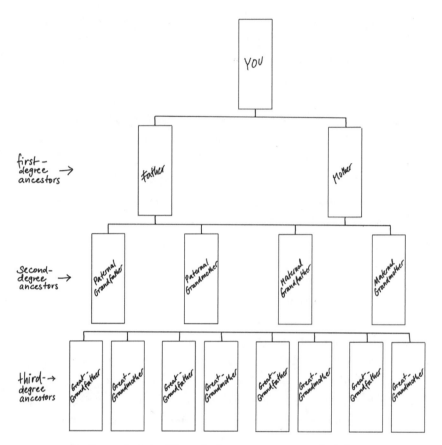

Family tree depicting "degrees" of genetic transmission. Each degree
requires a new level of attunement for ancestral healing.

Sometimes, the consonance between one's own life and an ancestor's past is both mysterious and undeniable. Niyati, the daughter of Holocaust survivors, departed the Netherlands by boat as a teenager. She was excited about the trip, but as the vessel sailed away, she found herself alone at the rear of the ship, overcome by incomprehensible grief. As she watched the shore disappear into the distance, Niyati shook with tears she could not explain.

Only decades later did Niyati learn of the agonizing day in May of 1940, when her grandmother, Claire, escaped the Nazis by taking the last boat to England out of the Dutch port of Ijmuiden, the same point of departure that her granddaughter took many years later. Claire's family had raced with thousands of other Jews to make it aboard the ship, but in the chaos, her husband and only daughter were separated from her and did not make it out of the country in time. Realizing this terrible fact, Oma Claire had stood alone at the stern of the vessel, watching the shores of Holland shrink on the horizon, stricken with unfathomable grief that her family was now lost to her and paralyzed by the terrible knowledge of what surely awaited them.

Whether or not we ever discover, as Niyati finally did, the biographical details that allow us to connect our own pain to the pain of our predecessors, the fact remains: any unhealed trauma they suffered is *our* unhealed trauma. We may experience a pattern of toxic stress or a general sense of disconnection and unease. It may present itself in the form of unexplained fears or phobias, bouts of anxiety or depression, or any other difficult emotion that appears to be out of sync with our current experience.

As I wrote in *Healing Collective Trauma*, researchers continue to present compelling evidence for the epigenetic transmission of trauma. Some of the earliest studies on the multigenerational transmission of trauma were conducted on the descendants of Holocaust survivors, such as those led by Rachel Yehuda, PhD, director of the Traumatic Stress Studies Division at Mount Sinai School of Medicine. Although more research is needed, Yehuda's findings had a telling resonance for many communities and their genetic descendants across the world and for other groups who have suffered marked historical traumas resulting from war, genocide, slavery, and colonization.

Many of the intergenerational symptoms of trauma common to such groups only perpetuate further adversity and suffering for the community. These symptoms can include increased incidence of physical and psychological illness, a pattern of domestic disturbance, vulnerability to addiction, and poor outcomes for education and economic stability.

Despite the overwhelming evidence—plain for all who dare to look—
the question of intergenerational trauma is still a debated subject for
many in the sciences. Nevertheless, daring scientists forge onward.

Kerry J. Ressler, a neurobiologist and psychiatrist at McLean
Hospital in Belmont, Massachusetts, and his colleague Brian Dias
co-authored a 2013 study, published in the journal *Nature.* As reporter
Ewen Callaway explained, Ressler "became interested in epigenetic
inheritance after working with poor people living in inner cities, where
cycles of drug addiction, neuropsychiatric illness, and other problems
often seem to recur in parents and their children."[3]

To examine the epigenetic inheritance of behavioral factors, the
researchers used laboratory mice, which they trained to fear the smell
of acetophenone, a chemical with a scent similar to cherries or almonds.
The researchers exposed a group of male mice to the acetophenone while
providing a small electric shock. The mice quickly learned to fear the
scent and behaved accordingly by quivering and otherwise demonstrating a visual stress response, whether or not the shocks were delivered.

No further shocks were administered to the original group of mice
or to their progeny. However, similar to Isabelle Mansuy's mice study
described in chapter 6, when each new generation (i.e., the grandchildren, great-grandchildren, and so on of the original group) was exposed
to the odor of acetophenone, those new mice exhibited the same stress
response that their predecessors had, becoming agitated, distressed,
and chaotic. This behavior response repeated for generations.

Unmetabolized trauma in the ancestral lineage creates a place of
disconnection, like a broken water pipe. Its presence impedes the flow
of light and information through the intergenerational tree or family
system. Downstream, these untended blockages beget dysfunctional
family relationships, which further damage familial bonds and result
in symptoms tellingly observed across many historically traumatized
cultural groups, in all parts of the world. Until the community's original ancestral wounds can be acknowledged and addressed, subsequent
generations will continue to bear the burden of historical crisis.

Wherever our parents, grandparents, or great-grandparents were fragmented by adversity, the signature of that fragmentation lives on in their nervous systems. However silently, it shows up in our bodies, our behaviors, our emotional structures, and, therefore, in our relationships. This is what makes ancestral integration work so important and so urgent. After all, we live in times that demand the healthiest, sanest, wisest, and most deeply related humans we can be.

DR. EDUARDO DURAN ON INDIGENOUS COMMUNITY
HEALING AND THE FOURTEEN GENERATIONS CONCEPT

Excerpted from Dr. Duran's talks during the Collective Trauma Summit 2021[4]

Early on in my work with Indigenous communities, when sitting with a person, a couple, or a family, I found that during the time I spoke with them, I began to have the feeling that there was someone else in the [room] with us. But as soon as my clients would leave, the feeling would go away.

This feeling got stronger and stronger over time, until I thought, *Well, maybe there's a problem with me. Maybe I'm too stressed. The graduate work is making me think things.* But it just kept getting stronger, and I had no context for it. I couldn't very well attend to this feeling in front of my patients—that there's something else in the room no one could see. That would be out of line. I was starting to think I was in the wrong field. *I just need to go back to the military where things make sense and I don't get this feeling,* I thought.

But one day, a traditional doctor (medicine person) showed up. I had never met him before, but I understood [from the community] that his medicine was very powerful. I was told you wouldn't even have to tell him your dreams; he could tell *you* what you dreamed, and then he could tell you what the dream meant.

Wow! I thought. Even with Carl Jung, you had to tell him your dream first. So, I was pretty nervous, and I didn't know why he was here. But since I couldn't tell my clinical supervisor about the feelings I was experiencing—for obvious reasons—I decided maybe I could tell the medicine person. I thought, *Well, even if he reports me, nobody's going to believe him. He's a trance doctor, and people are going to think he's crazy, so it's safe.* [laughing] So, I told him what I was experiencing. I was hoping that he would tell me I just needed to take some time off and have a rest.

He did the exact opposite. "The reason you're having this feeling," he said, "is because there *are* others there."

"*Who?!*" I asked.

He explained that over a thirty-year period, between 1870 and 1900, among the communities I was working with *80 percent* of all the Native people had been exterminated, genocided militarily and [by infectious disease] biological warfare.

And when that happens, he explained, a sudden genocide like that, the [souls of the] people don't have time to cross over and be in harmony among the ancestors. Because of natural law, he said, the only place that this healing can happen is here, in the same place where the injury occurred.

He told me that what I was experiencing were the ancestors and the unborn ones of the people I was working with. They were showing up to our therapy sessions, hoping that their living relatives could begin to heal themselves because their healing would be passed to those in the spirit world. Most of the Indigenous communities I have visited all over the world have a similar belief. That everything we do affects seven generations.

"In spirit time and in dreamtime, time doesn't only move forward," the medicine man told me. "It can also move backward." This meant that seven generations before and seven generations after—that's fourteen generations—have come together in that moment. [They enter from] the sacred seventh direction, the center of the heart, which is where the medicine is released . . . so that the ancestors can be released.

And this allows the unborn ones to say, "We don't have to repeat this when we come in."

If we do the healing work now, those who are born seven generations from now won't ever need to have this conversation. That's the genesis of the fourteen generations idea.

ACKNOWLEDGING THE ANCESTORS

Imago Relationship Therapy, developed in 1980 by Harville Hendrix and Helen LaKelly Hunt, is premised on the idea that many couples are initially attracted to one another on the basis of their unhealed family wounds.[5] *Imago*, taken from the Latin for "image," refers to "the unconscious image of familiar love." In his book on the subject, Hendrix proposed that an overwhelming spark of attraction felt between strangers is often based in an unconscious recognition of shared trauma. Any relationship that unfolds from such a connection is often plagued with difficulty, yet the struggle is precisely what is needed to help both individuals (and perhaps by extension, their community of ancestors and descendants) to recognize and work to heal their familial wounds. As we have seen again and again, the beauty of unhealed pain is that its symptoms will continually resurface, again and again, reminding us to tend our wounds and repair our lives.

When you think of your ancestors, they may feel very close to your heart. Perhaps you think and speak of them regularly and even feel their presence in your life or your children's lives. You may have familial customs and rituals for honoring the ancestors on sacred days of the year, when you mindfully offer up gratitude and acknowledgement for their contributions in your life.

For many in contemporary society, however, the notion of the ancestors can feel quite remote or abstract. When they think of their predecessors, if they do at all, they feel distant, as though merely a far-away notion and not a living energy. This is especially common when one's ancestors were known to harbor attitudes, beliefs, or behaviors that are considered problematic or even deeply unethical today.

Ancestral healing is not always easy, of course. Often we are dealing with deep trauma, broken family systems, or legacies of social oppression, which may involve the crimes of war, violence, and power abuses. The scars that such injuries leave behind are not easily reconciled and require that we look skillfully and with competence at the residue of the past. The important thing is that we do it. We must.

Psychotherapeutic approaches have come a long way in many respects. Childhood trauma and attachment models are finally coming into focus for the mainstream. They show us how essential models of healthy relating are for human development, personality formation, and physical and mental health over the lifespan. With this foundation, however, it is time that we broaden the map to include deeper spheres of systemic human function and webs of connection.

WOUNDED ANCESTORS

Whether or not we agree with our ancestors' choices, we nonetheless inherit the shadows that they did not illuminate in their lifetimes. In these circumstances, the journey to reveal and acknowledge our familial past is vital, even and especially when it reveals the perpetration of violence. This work requires skill and care, and it must be approached at the right pace. The unsettled conflicts and moral wounds of the past are extant in our living bodies. To resolve and integrate complicated human legacies requires that we carefully and consciously attend to the numbed, distant, and absent places within. Simply choosing not to know, feel, or reckon with the truth of who we once were is a decision to keep the truth hidden in darkness. It is only by the light of conscious awareness that we illuminate the shadows and catalyze healing integration.

I have worked with many German descendants of Nazi officers and soldiers, and I have seen how difficult it can be for people to acknowledge and meet with their ancestral past. Distancing, absencing, and denial are common defenses against the "sins of the fathers." But by refusing to awaken to the consequences of the ancestor's choices, we both suffer and perpetuate them.

When working with people whose ancestors perpetrated violence, whether individually or in groups, a large part of that work must be focused on the natural defenses such as denial. The key is to not make their denial, or any other defensive strategy, "wrong"; the defense is not the enemy. Our aim is simply to encourage people to stay with it and to explore what happens when we look together with care at the fact that we don't want to feel our ancestors or acknowledge their past actions.

Importantly, we need not agree with or condone the harmful beliefs or behaviors of our ancestors to acknowledge their contributions to our lives. This is a point of considerable conflict for many, yet deep down we know the paradoxical truth: our ancestors gave us life, and that is sacred. As long as we refuse to acknowledge their past moral failures, those past moral failures repeat in the form of our own living struggles and social crises. It is only by choosing to witness and digest our ancestor's crimes that we have the power to stop them from being repeated.

Whatever we choose *not* to hold in awareness runs us and thereby becomes our destiny. No matter how much we suppress and avoid and deny, the shadows are unavoidable. When we carry unacknowledged familial or historical traumas, our ancestors are not in peace. As a result, our living nervous systems—and, therefore, our minds and bodies—cannot maintain a healthy state of flow. The stream of energy and information that gets channeled through the human system is blocked, diminished, and distorted. Though it may be true that we cannot change history, by creating ancestral intimacy we *can* change its effects on the present.

CHOOSING HOW TO RELATE TO EXPERIENCE

If I decide that I will *never* become like my father, I am, in effect, choosing what I don't want to be because it is too painful—and that choice will bind me to the qualities of my father that I dislike. I will likely exhibit those very qualities but remain unconscious of them or their consequences in my life.

If I consciously choose a new relationship *to my experience* of my father, however, I may discover more freedom in how to express what my father has passed on to me. This choice illuminates the strengths and gifts that are available and creates a new potential for healing within my family story.

Opening the door to relation with the ancestors can be challenging. It is difficult to own what they could not. But by courageously opening ourselves to the truth of their lives with the intention to integrate even our most difficult histories, we and all our relations throughout time begin to awaken together into a more illuminated world. This simple act of presence makes way for new choices, new possibilities, new futures, and new light—for ourselves, our children, and their children.

The natural or divine law determines the flow of energy throughout hundreds of thousands of years of life. Karma is just the postponement of experience. Integration is the act of clearing karma so that light, energy, wisdom, and strength are transmitted to future generations—and perhaps even to prior ones.

DR. LAURA CALDERÓN DE LA BARCA ON RACISM, MEMORY, AND THE INVITATION

Laura Calderón de la Barca, PhD, is a psychotherapist, cultural analyst, author, and educator from Mexico. She assists the Timeless Wisdom Training and is a valued member of The Pocket Project, an international non-profit organization whose mission is to contribute to the healing of collective and intergenerational trauma, and to reduce its disruptive effects on our global culture.

I am of mixed ancestry, part indigenous and part Spanish, and I grew up in an environment that was a higher level within my society than the one my parents were born to. They worked very hard to get themselves to an economically better place, and that gave them access to better schools for their children than those they attended as children. So, my parents opened a door for us, but they were less equipped to provide us the social guidance for how to navigate those spaces.

The school I attended belonged largely to the upper middle class. One day, when I was about nine years old, I remember arriving to school and walking in with my school bag. As I passed through the gate, an older boy was standing there—a white boy. And as I walked by, the boy approached me and hissed in my ear. *"Negra!"*

The moment he said that to me, a massive energy erupted inside my body. Today, I would call it shame. Suddenly, my heart was pounding, and my breathing was shallow. I started to walk very quickly. I wanted to get away from him—away from the scene and anybody who might have witnessed it. I could feel the tears burning in my eyes, but I would *not* allow myself to cry. Crying would have made my shame so much worse; it would show everyone that the boy's curse had affected me. If that happened, I would feel like a failure.

I did not fully understand this at the time, but crying would feel like a betrayal of my family, of my lineage. My tears would communicate that I thought I had no right to be there at that school when I knew I had every right to be—just as much right as the boy. I was, of course, filled with anger, too, and with wounded pride. And with grief—so much grief. My heart had broken in that moment, and I couldn't stop shaking for a long time.

I felt that I couldn't share what had happened with anybody, so I didn't. When I got to my classroom, I did what I have so often done, which was to bury myself behind a book and to try to look like I was busy, even though I was trying so hard not to cry. In the shock of that experience, I had dissociated. Being able to share this experience with you now is the result of a very long journey.

Later, when I was doing my PhD, I remember telling my PhD supervisor about the experience. "I understand that this was a very painful thing for you," he said. "But I can't quite make sense of the level of reaction I see in you now. Your reaction feels way bigger than what actually happened."

My supervisor's response felt like an opening for me, an opportunity for me to notice that I wasn't persecuted by that experience. My life hadn't been at risk—that was true. And acknowledging this became a point of entry: questioning the intensity of my personal experience led me to discover the layers of *collective* experience, ancestral and cultural, that I carry. That we all carry as part of us.

I'm part indigenous to Mexico; I have indigenous ancestors. They were not just discriminated against but persecuted and abused for being who they were. And my sense today is that this historical, ancestral part of me was resonating in my body when I erupted in pain and anger as that nine-year-old girl.

Although I don't have direct African lineage, my ancestors witnessed and experienced in many ways—or participated in—what people of African ancestry endured. So, when a white boy used that particular slur, one associated with the Black community, to insult me, a part of me felt terror. Learning to see this has been difficult and painful; it meant seeing how a piece of that systemic racism story also lives in me. I'm not proud of that at all, which is why I feel it is so important to look. If I refuse to see it, then I have betrayed my lineage by allowing that story to continue in me. That is the invitation.

GIFTS OF THE ANCESTORS

The beauty of multigenerational healing work is in the profound discovery that ancestors are, in fact, our greatest resource. Their strengths, skills, talents, resourcefulness, ingenuity, resilience, and wisdom are available to us in the present. By attending to the injuries within our ancestral lines, we make new space for the gifts of ancestry to be revealed and awakened. And we can harvest those gifts and resources to engage deeper ancestral healing. In the process, we come to feel more deeply supported and more powerfully connected in ways that transcend time or place. Healing is only the beginning, you see. The true reward of ancestral restoration, or any other collective trauma integration process, is the power it has to shift our awareness from "me" to "we," from individual focus to collective awakening.

You are your ancestors' future. When you allow yourself to really feel the past, not just to think about it, you discover that you have the power to sync the fragmented past and the unhealed trauma of your lineage with the present moment. Every time you do this, frozen energy from the past gets released and integrated into the lifestream. This is a powerful healing force; it allows the future to change the past. You can cohere the individual, ancestral, and collective nervous system and sync the past with the present, releasing the pain that your ancestors were forced to suppress just to survive. By restoring and integrating the collective past, you generate new learning and wisdom for today.

When your ancestors are at peace, you are at peace.

As you begin to address the legacy of fragmentation that was passed on to you, your life changes, and those changes ripple outward. The healing extends backward in time as the retrocausal liberation of the ancestors and unfolds forward in time as greater potential and possibility for the future lives of your descendants. What's more, the radiant and scintillating energies of restoration begin to spread outward into your community, affecting at the subtlest level everyone you know and many you do not.

When your ancestors are at peace, you are at peace.

Ancestral healing innervates the collective nervous system and restores light throughout the whole. This light is required to generate new and necessary structures of consciousness, including those that will allow humanity to remember and repair our sacred connection to the earth and all other life-forms. It is incumbent upon us to transform collective suffering into unification, integration, and love. In fact, I believe it is a vital part of our purpose.

PRACTICE: A SIMPLE ANCESTRAL HEALING

Ancestral healing can be approached as an inner contemplative journey. With care and awareness, the living has the power to help restore ancestral or intergenerational trauma energies by bringing it back into presence and integration. This generates new learning, posttraumatic growth, and resilience within your lineage, which ripples out to positively impact others in your community. If you find this process challenging, please only do so in the presence of a skilled therapist or in a facilitated group setting.

First, find a quiet time and place where you won't be disturbed, and get comfortable.

When you're ready, connect to your own body by attuning to your inner sensations, thoughts, and feelings. You will use this inner awareness as the instrument of connection.

Next, set a clear intention to connect to a specific ancestor or ancestors. As you do, know that your body's nervous system is able to tune in to information about the ancestor, wherever this wisdom lives in your family or story. Simply listen and make space to receive, while loosely holding your intention with soft concentration.

Notice whatever sensation, emotion, image, atmosphere, taste, or memory shows up. Now, stay with your impression by tuning in more deeply. Often, the impression will deepen, revealing more of itself to you. It's important to stay with the unfolding information as it is, without trying to interpret or understand it.

Some find it helpful to journal about the process, as writing can foster an intuitive stream of information and awareness. Remember not to fixate on an interpretation; instead, simply be present and notice what is.

Thinking only about the trauma will neither move nor shift it; *feeling* and *sensing* the trauma information is needed. Intergenerational healing occurs when you bring presence and relationality to the split or fragmented energies of trauma so that they can be reintegrated back into the river of life.

SENSING VERSUS IMAGINING THE ANCESTORS

There is a vital difference between *imagining* a client's ancestors and fundamentally *sensing* information brought forward about their ancestors. You might have some prior knowledge of or even just an imagined version of the ancestors, but what you really need can only be found with intentional attunement, simply by noticing what arises in the body, the mind, or the emotions as you think about and tune in with the ancestors.

When you tune in to your own great-grandmother, for example, what do you notice in your body? In your emotions? What inner images or thoughts arise? Once you tune into the first feeling, sensation, or image, you are then given access to other, more deeply stored information. Even if the only feeling you can perceive is numbness or absence, that is precisely the information you need to work with.

10

Healing for the Collective

The feeling-tone of the body scores the symphony of consciousness . . .
—MARIA POPOVA

We never know what we can become for others through our Being.
—MARTIN HEIDEGGER

When you encounter a virus, a toxin, or merely a common environmental allergen, your body's immune system expresses an initial reaction to the potential threat, triggering a cascade of intelligent immune responses designed to ensure your survival and return you to wellness. These are exquisite evolutionary mechanisms, refined over millions of years.

The same is true for the human collective. As a complex system, a collective possesses self-similarity; essential characteristics belonging to individuals are replicated at scale across human groups (organizations, communities, societies, and humanity at large). Human systems also possess an evolutionary self-healing, self-balancing immune function. There's a brilliantly orchestrated order within the larger system, lying just beneath the surface of human awareness. And like walking antibodies or white blood cells, we each participate in the collective immune function, albeit in ways we may never fully recognize or comprehend.

Just as your body's immune response can potentially overcorrect or backfire—essentially defeating its intended purpose by becoming overreactive and attacking the body itself—so, too, can the collective immune system. Remember, trauma isn't the shocking thing that happened to you; it's your *reaction* to what happened to you. You can get so caught up in your reactions to real or perceived threats that you fail to appropriately meet and digest your reactions. Or worse, *you* can become the threat. And it is much the same with communities—or even nations.

In early 2022, Europe's largest land war since the Second World War broke out inside the borders of Ukraine. In only the first few weeks of conflict, an estimated 3.2 million people fled the country, with many more to follow. In addition to the swell of migrants flooding into Poland, Slovakia, Hungary, Romania, and elsewhere, there were an estimated 6.5 million internally displaced persons (IDPs) by the third week of conflict,[1] people still within Ukraine who were unable to remain in their homes, cities, or regions due to the invasion of their homeland by Russian armed forces. Many among them had been forcibly displaced during Russia's 2014 invasion of the Donbas region and annexation of Crimea. In short order, countless Ukrainian citizens and others living within its borders became refugees of war—some not for the first time—and the central subjects of a growing humanitarian crisis.

According to the United Nations Refugee Agency, by the end of 2020, 82.4 million people worldwide were dislocated from their homes and communities due to "persecution, conflict, violence, human rights violations, or events seriously disturbing public order."[2] Like the growing number of war refugees fleeing Ukraine—the majority of whom are women, children, and the elderly—displaced people are said to encounter four broad categories of trauma: *traumatic stress, acculturation stress, resettlement stress*, and *isolation*.[3] Even when migrants manage to safely cross national borders (no guarantee) and find temporary or longer-term safe shelter (also no guarantee), their trauma is not over. In many ways, it may only just be starting.

Given the increasing volatility, uncertainty, complexity, and ambiguity of contemporary life, we must consider the compounding nature of other large-scale social challenges.

I began this book with a bird's-eye view of what is perhaps the greatest civilizational crisis of our time, the global ecological emergency. Climate change has and will continue to produce an inestimable number of refugees, mass migrations of people forced to flee accelerating natural disasters—floods, fires, famine, disease, and other hazards—in climate "hot spots" around the world. Already, we have seen large numbers of climate-displaced persons across the Americas, Africa, Europe, Asia, Australia, and elsewhere—and the numbers are only expected to grow,[4] perhaps exponentially.

The central truth that brings us here is this: wherever they go, displaced persons bring the trauma of their experiences with them, and sadly they will be met by many new ones. As I've said, within the collective unconscious, there is a large-scale trauma field that connects us all. It links every Venezuelan to every Kazakhstani, every Senegalese to every Swede. Any instance of conflict or adversity in one country is intimately related to every other because the trauma that is felt by any one of us lives within all of us.

Likewise, we are all part of the same Earth, and anywhere there is ecological suffering—from ravaged rain forests burning in the Amazon to plastic- and chemical-choked coral reefs in Indonesia—that suffering belongs to everyone. Despite our illusion of separateness, we are, in fact, one world. Interconnectedness is not an idealistic metaphor but an immutable fact. And because we are so profoundly interlinked, all who are able have a duty to learn to activate the collective immune system and awaken together the human capacity to meet the incredible challenges and wicked problems of our time. To solve even one systemic problem will require much more than careful planning and strategic action. If *un*conscious patterns are the fundamental substance of systemic breakdowns, only clear and activated consciousness can be brought to bear to address them.

First and foremost, we must be willing to presence and witness, to *feel* and *sense* and *see*, the manifestations of shadow, ignorance, and trauma within ourselves and others. On the surface, this can seem daunting or even unnecessary. Consensus culture, which is rife with systemic breakdown, would have us believe that such notions are frivolous, impractical, and pointless. Yet, this position is itself symptomatic of a traumatized society, which induces the slumber from which we must awaken.

To understand the urgency we face, consider what happens when we refuse to acknowledge, much less to presence, the symptoms presented by our collective shadow. "In the archetypal psychotherapy that I practice," writes spiritual author and psychotherapist Thomas Moore, "we always say: Go with the symptom. I don't look for quick escapes from the pain or good distracting alternatives. I try to imagine how a symptom . . . might be reimagined and even lived out in a [new] way."[5] Symptoms are echoes of the original trauma, part of a process that has become stuck in time and space. Our work is to go deeper and discover the origin of the echo so that it can finally be healed.

Ninety years before Ukraine's sovereignty was invaded in the 2022 Russo-Ukrainian war, an atrocity of incomprehensible proportions took place there, one whose dark shadow still binds Ukraine to its Russian neighbors and relatives. In the Holodomor,[6] or Terror Famine, millions of ethnic Ukrainians were starved to death within a year, an act of genocide engineered by Soviet dictator Joseph Stalin.[7]

In 1932–1933 Ukraine, the devastation of the Holodomor was visible everywhere. Yet for half a century, the Soviet Union denied the famine had ever taken place, labeling any mention of the Holodomor as "anti-Soviet propaganda." In fact, all information about the famine and the millions who died as a result was so suppressed that no official public mention of the event occurred until 1987.[8] In all that time, Ukrainians were expected to deny or forget how their own people—their ancestors, loved ones, community members, and countrymen—had been callously exterminated.

Scholars argue the Holodomor was Stalin's brutal and extreme attempt to quash Ukrainian independence. Others claim that famine was the appalling result of widespread apathy, bureaucratic incompetence, and the Communist Party's collectivization efforts, in which the government seized the lands, personal property, and many homes of poor farmers and agricultural workers, thereby eradicating Ukrainian self-sufficiency and plunging the region into worsening food shortages, inevitable starvation, and social catastrophe.

The Holodomor was not the first horror to befall the Ukrainian people, nor the last to occur in the intervening century, but its example is illustrative and important to apprehend. Whatever Stalin's motivation or the true cause of the atrocity, it isn't difficult to detect the underlying themes still present in the region today, even if those energies remain largely in shadow. In truth, war is never a problem of misaligned political or economic interests. It is the consequence of rejected shadow and the disowned, unattended wounds of the past, which must by their nature resurface time and again until we collectively agree to acknowledge and amend them.

GLOBAL SOCIAL WITNESSING

War isn't new; violent conflict is an ancient, disrelational habit familiar to nearly all human societies. What *is* new about war and other mass-traumatization events in the twenty-first century is the presence of the internet and social media—namely, the ease and power of so many to upload images and videos from the battlefield in real time.

For the first time in human history, wherever we are and no matter how far away, we can witness and react to what's happening in active conflict zones or disaster scenes a world away. Even if we choose to avoid social media and online or television news, it can be difficult for most people to miss what's happening around them. Bad news, like gossip, is pervasive—and it *spreads*, an adaptive evolutionary strategy that promotes survival, though if prolonged, promotes social dysfunction and breakdown. Despite the unprecedented access to information now available, we are often not so much well informed as we are overwhelmed. And if not overwhelmed, we're likely desensitized, numb, cynical, or shut down.

Modern media sensationalizes news of violence, threat, and danger, profiting off human fear and furthering societal polarization. The massive onslaught of polarizing data we consume is not immediately digestible. In fact, unfettered access to information about active trauma may create what researchers have called secondhand or vicarious traumatization, especially for the highly empathetic person.[9] At the very least, constant news of human struggle, violence, and adversity can result in burnout and compassion fatigue. Yet, the more anesthetized we become to the suffering of others, the less capable we are of responding with discernment and wise action to help end or prevent further suffering in the world. Without knowing it, we may become complicit in the ongoing repetition of humanity's darkest cultural traumas through unconscious activation of the hidden energies that make trauma possible in the first place.

WHAT WOULD TRAUMA-INFORMED MEDIA LOOK LIKE?

Sensational news headlines and divisive online engagement activate trauma patterns within the collective unconscious, amplifying apathy and indifference at one end and heightening emotional disruption at the other. News media websites and social media apps are coded for "increased engagement," because more clicks mean more dollars for shareholders. To support this unwieldy and unethical financial model, artificial intelligence algorithms are designed to push ever more extreme controversy, fear, and antagonism, thereby privileging "incendiary content, [and] setting up a stimulus–response loop that promotes outrage expression."[10]

The end result has been increased social polarization and conflict, poor mental health outcomes, and further extremes in economic inequity. Is it any wonder that depression, anxiety, addiction, and self-harm are exploding among young people?

What would trauma-informed media look like? It's a question that deserves critical research. What's clear is that contemporary societies need to focus at least as much attention on healing and health as they do on increasing gross domestic product. Imagine a new media and economic landscape that is grounded, professional, and ethical, whose leaders value human health above personal profit. Imagine global news media that engenders wider understanding and compassion *as* it informs us.

You see, collective trauma is not an academic abstraction or even a sociological concept. In the most real sense, it is the mass of unmetabolized energy that exists within and all around us as a result of toxic stress, adversity, shock, and trauma. Even if we don't know it's there, the energy of mass trauma affects us—all of us. It shapes our lives and alters our relationships, our communities, and the natural world around us. There is nothing left untouched by collective trauma. In fact, its nature is so ubiquitous and its effects so insidious that we have come to consider it "normal." *This is just how things are. Just how families are. Just how people are. Just how the world is.*

Yet nothing could be further from the truth. Integration allows us to harvest the frozen, disclaimed energies of the past and use them to illuminate our perspective in the present.

As the great German writer, scientist, and statesman Johann Wolfgang von Goethe observed, "Man knows himself only to the extent that he knows the world; he becomes aware of himself only within the world and aware of the world only within himself. Every new object, well contemplated, opens up a new organ of perception in us."[11] By opening ourselves to the exploration of trauma's effects within and around us, we come to know more of ourselves, the world, and one another. After all, only what we acknowledge can be integrated—and the integration of trauma becomes posttraumatic learning.

What's more, healing the ethical transgressions of the past develops our ethical understanding today. This wisdom is vital if we wish to meet contemporary ethical challenges: from questions about artificial intelligence, nano tech, genetic engineering, cyberwarfare, new weapons of mass destruction, and other evolutionary concerns. Perhaps one day, a mandate to reckon with and heal historical and collective trauma will be written into the constitutions of nations.

To begin to address the phenomenon of collective trauma at its source, I developed an awareness-based practice called Global Social Witnessing (GSW). GSW is a social mindfulness practice that shows us the limits of our capacity to be a present witness to events—including and especially to traumatic events—that are reported within society. Through sustained practice of GSW, we begin to see into the gaps, the places where we may intellectually understand the facts of the news stories we consume, but where we become emotionally or even physically stressed and overwhelmed by the contents or where we alternately shut down and numb, potentially unaware that relation has been lost. When this occurs, we are no longer in witness. The gap itself represents the distance (or incongruence) between one's interior and exterior and contains the unprocessed collective trauma we carry within. We practice GSW to help make the collective trauma field more visible so that, step-by-step, we can begin to integrate the internal fragmentation we all carry.

In its simplest form, GSW is the act of consciously presencing, witnessing, sensing, and feeling into the dense energies of adverse current events—whether the stream of alarming news stories pouring into your daily newsfeed or the sudden outbreak of war in Eastern Europe. Global Social Witnessing can be initiated as an individual practice or facilitated in a group context, even with very large groups. And it is meant to be used in a titrated fashion; as practitioners, we take on one adverse current event at a time.

To address trauma, we must meet it at the root. We must engage in a practice of making conscious that which is unconscious. We must choose to notice, feel, and digest the energies we otherwise instinctively resist, suppress, avoid, disown, and deny. Global Social Witnessing is a practice for *being with* the difficult energies of the large-scale traumatic events occurring in the world around us: ongoing wars in nations like Afghanistan, Syria, Yemen, Ethiopia, and elsewhere; the mounting cartel violence in South and Central America; continuing civil unrest, armed violence, and human rights abuses in Burkina Faso, Cameroon, Myanmar, the Republic of Congo, and beyond; the oppression and genocide of the Uyghur people of China; and the many other human and planetary wounds that call out for our care and attention. Without our care and attention, these compounding traumas will continue unabated. Human rights can only be honored and preserved through genuine relatedness. It is the lack of relatedness that makes the violation of human rights possible.

Global Social Witnessing is a form of dialogic inquiry—defined by one scholar as "the tool kit of discourse in the activity of learning"[12]—in which, together, we presence the collective field so as to mindfully attend to global events with embodied awareness. In practice, GSW is a model that allows us to make visible the invisible forces that influence our lives in order that we may apprehend and transform them.

PRACTICE: GLOBAL SOCIAL WITNESSING

Search for a disquieting piece of news about current events—a headline or news article, for example—to bring into your practice. It should be information that's difficult or upsetting, without being too overwhelming.

The story you choose could be about a school shooting, a local act of violence, or a story about climate change—whatever feels important to focus on.

Now sit down, and as you read the news headline, check in with your body, noticing any sensations, feelings, images, or impressions that arise. Are you reading the headline intellectually but feeling emotionally or physically numb or disconnected? Do you experience an activation of fear, stress, or upset? Or do you notice a sense of felt connection to the event?

The point of the practice is not to be able to feel or sense the event; the point is to see our limitations. We practice GSW in order to become aware of our "edge," where the capacity for being an embodied witness stops.

The end of your ability to sense and feel marks the beginning of the collective unconscious or collective absence. The overwhelming nature of the information reduces the function of collective witnessing, or presence, so that the energy of these events doesn't get processed or reconciled and must, therefore, repeat.

Widespread use of the internet and mobile devices makes us think of ourselves as super informed, yet numbness, absence, and overwhelm are all too common. These responses to collective trauma prevent us from fully metabolizing the information we experience. However, we can all be more mindful about how we consume the news and engage in the Three-Sync Practice as we do so.

A GSW practice can also be powerful in groups, where members of the group share their inner experience with others who bring their attunement, presence, and witness to the whole.

Global Social Witnessing invites us to align our individual interiors within a wider collective and intersubjective container. When we practice, it is our shared intention to tune into self and other—and to the interior and exterior worlds at the same time. The practice of GSW strengthens our capacity to host the Other within, to embrace the Other with a shared heart. Through the GSW practice, we become more mature global citizens, better equipped to co-create new ideas and approaches for transforming the dense energies of disruption into the vitality of future innovation.

As global citizens, it is incumbent upon us to express global citizenship. We must also recognize the fundamental human responsibility we share, which is to practice making conscious the dark energies of human suffering so that those energies can be digested, integrated, and returned to the life flow of future potential. Whole states must address the social wounds created by war, colonialism, racism, anti-Semitism, gender violence, and environmental degradation. When done in earnest, this work restores the flow of light, or conscious awareness, to the collective body and makes healthier and more sustainable societies possible.

Gus Speth, the American environmental lawyer and former US senior advisor on climate change, has said, "I used to think that top environmental problems were biodiversity loss, ecosystem collapse, and climate change. I thought that thirty years of good science could address these problems. I was wrong. The top environmental problems are selfishness, greed, and apathy, and to deal with these we need a cultural and spiritual transformation."[13]

Speth is right, of course, though it's important to note that the selfishness, greed, and apathy he mentions are, in truth, only *symptoms* of the larger problem, which is our unaddressed collective shadow and unhealed collective trauma. It is our willingness to awaken to, experience, and transform these root causes that creates the cultural and spiritual transformation Speth prescribes.

We can think of the global immune system as a refined resonance capacity. It represents the most essential, ancient, and evolutionary wisdom for dealing with the reactive mental, emotional, and psychosocial aspects that arise within us in response to the traumatic residue and accelerating disruption all around us.

Regardless of how far removed we may be physically from unfolding unrest or atrocities—in Ukraine, Yemen, Ethiopia, Haiti, Myanmar, Israel, Palestine, and elsewhere—we are no less affected by them. And it is precisely because we are touched by these events that we have the power to help shift them. Collective healing starts with the immune reaction, the experiences that come up inside us when we're faced with the realities on the ground or in media reports and images shared during active conflict. Even as distant observers, we can feel disturbed and activated by these events, which can show up in many forms: fear, terror, anger, outrage, numbness, or shutting down.

Yet it's our power to simultaneously *feel* and *witness* our feelings and reactions that allows us to digest and integrate some measure of the overall trauma energy. This is the collective immune response in its most conscious and participatory state. And it is vitally urgent that we learn to engage in collective self-healing.

The global immune system is the organ through which we become activated by disturbance in the field, but it's also the instrument through which we may more consciously attune to the world around us in order to integrate that disturbance and restore balance to the living system. Only a small number of us—a critical mass, if you will—is required to engage before a new level of collective coherence becomes established in sympathetic resonance, ringing like a tuning fork across the field, inviting the entire world to join.

INTEGRATING COLLECTIVE TRAUMA FOR WORLD HEALING

Many are beginning to recognize the ways that unhealed personal trauma can harm development and manifest in long-term suffering and relational problems. What is perhaps less well understood is how unaddressed collective trauma places a similar burden on the health and development of human communities, cultures, organizations, institutions, and societies. To the extent that we observe injury, imbalance, corruption, or decay in our schools, religious institutions, businesses, health-care systems, infrastructure, and environment, we are seeing the wider impact of unaddressed collective wounds.

As I wrote in *Healing Collective Trauma*, it is my belief that unresolved systemic and multigenerational traumas delay the development of the human family, injure the natural world, and forestall the higher evolution of our species. *Not* to address the hidden wounds of the collective human body is to place our planet further in peril and the survival of our own species at grave risk.

> Not *to address the hidden wounds of the collective human body is to place our planet further in peril and the survival of our own species at grave risk.*

Through many years facilitating group-change processes, including those between large groups of Germans and Israelis—two groups with a well-known legacy of traumatic interrelations—I arrived at a method for guiding people through a profoundly healing awareness-based process, the Collective Trauma Integration Process (CTIP).[14] The methodology behind CTIP unfolded through the sincere and illuminating efforts of every participant (and there have now been many thousands), the devoted therapeutic assistance of those who've joined me in the facilitation process and careful study of the pioneering research and groundbreaking science of trauma.

From chapter 8, you'll recall that the goal of CTIP is to help us witness, experience, and integrate our shared cultural and historical traumas. The core of CTIP, the first and most fundamental ingredient necessary for the fulfillment of that goal, is the relational coherence of the group. Everything depends on group cohesion, which is not the same as participant "sameness" and isn't dependent on familiarity among group members. Relational coherence is an expression of shared intention and embodied awareness, and it is a product of skilled facilitation. When true coherence emerges, the group's higher collective intelligence or wisdom is activated and takes shape in ways we could not plan for or construct beforehand. In this way, CTIP is a fundamentally *emergent* process of group consciousness, mutual relatedness, and shared witness. We might think of it as a "we-space" practice, because it is.

The CTIP model unfolds through six core stages, or waves:

> **Wave 1:** Relational coherence is created and sustained through embodied awareness and guided transpersonal facilitation.

> **Wave 2:** As we presence the field with the intention of sensing collective trauma, symptoms of denial or repression of the trauma begin to surface in members of the group. For example, some people may start to yawn or lose focus. Others might notice they feel sleepy or even irritable. These qualities are understood as symptoms of our resistance to the trauma. As symptoms appear among group participants, we take gentle notice of them together with the aim of staying present to whatever arises.

> **Wave 3:** As the energy of resistance is processed and cleared, a new and more powerful wave of energy can enter. This wave often takes the form of an eruption of energy related to the collective trauma we're gathered to address. Strong emotions may be felt by participants, and historical or ancestral group memories may surface.

> **Wave 4:** As we process these energies together, certain participants become a conduit for the collective past to be voiced, expressed, acknowledged, and witnessed by the whole. Together, we track the specificity of these individual and collective voices, which clarify our work and help guide us in the process.

> **Wave 5:** (small-group work) Members are led in the Three-Sync Practice to align the body, mind, and emotions. Group integration work begins.

Wave 6: (metaprocess) The small groups come back together as one for a period of further sharing, transpersonal witnessing, and group integration.

For the CTIP to be done safely and effectively, skilled assistants are on hand to aid anyone who may become overwhelmed by the emotions that can surface. When I facilitate CTIP groups, trained therapists who work alongside me are always present and available to provide anyone who needs or desires it with one-on-one support until they feel ready to rejoin the group. This is essential to the ethical stewardship of group-trauma integration.

The above is a highly condensed description of a vastly deeper group presencing practice. Facilitating the CTIP often takes place over a period of several days because a skillful process of this scale requires care and time; it isn't generally suited to contemporary culture's quick-fix desires. (I have been asked to submit articles for mainstream news out-lets in the vein of "Five Easy Steps You Can Take to Heal Community Trauma." I wish it were so simple.) Depth work rarely can be done in a single afternoon. Still, it's always humbling to witness the healing that's possible in even just a week's time, especially considering the historical scale of the wounds we gather to address.

The CTIP model was developed with the science of trauma in mind, and it is facilitated by the following principles:

Prevention is our first aim. As we better understand the nature and effects of collective trauma, we can align more effectively as a global society to prevent the systemic disruptions that lead to this phenomenon in the first place.

We owe it to future generations to address collective trauma in our world today. We must be willing to examine how ancestral, historical, and transgenerational traumas overlap and how they operate at the level of the collective unconscious, including the ways they shape many of our unquestioned social concepts, habits, and cultural agreements.

The long-term effects of collective trauma are not always obvious, and their source is not always clear. Many of the consequences do not appear in the immediate aftermath of the traumatic event; instead they unfold over time. Likewise, the source of trauma may not always be evident, as it would be in the case of a natural disaster or armed conflict. Instead, there may be multiple and complex social factors that play out over time and contribute to communal trauma, such as harmful policing practices, failing educational or health-care systems, or overburdened communities in crisis. (For example, historically traumatized communities are often the first and hardest hit by climate change and/or find themselves unduly burdened with problems of environmental injustice).

We must take special care to attend to and learn from the suffering—and the wisdom—of historically traumatized groups. While it's not the responsibility of these groups to educate others, we can partner in ways that benefit the whole, especially where sincere restorative-justice efforts are welcome and effective.

Although the effects of unresolved trauma can be severe, all people and collective human systems have a built-in mechanism for healing. When a safe, conscious, relational context is offered and trauma-informed care is present, healing can unfold and traumatic experiences can be transformed into resilience, strength, wisdom, and greater communal awakening.

Learning all we can about the near- and long-term impacts of trauma on people, families, communities, and societies helps prepare us to mitigate future crises and manifest radical new possibility. Trauma-informed people, communities, and cultures are far better equipped to transform the cultural forces and societal structures that otherwise promote further trauma.

At its heart, CTIP is a collective tool for sensing into the living field of consciousness and cohering the fragmented past. This work can help us do more than heal old wounds: it can awaken within us radically new human capacities and invite us more fully into the gifts of being and becoming—the profound result being the realization of deeper unity and a vibrant new space of collective intelligence and human unfolding.

ANCESTRAL RESOURCING

When trauma in an individual or a community is particularly severe, the prospect of healing change can seem far away or even impossible. However, any limitation in the potential for healing is itself a distortion because the body of every living human contains the accumulated insight and intelligence of countless millennia.

In a very real sense, your ancestors are present inside you. Without their existence, you would not be here. And while it's true that their untended traumas may have been passed on to you, it is equally true that their strength and resilience, their gifts and talents, their wisdom and insight are available within you now. Remember this as you proceed in the endeavor of ancestral healing—on behalf of yourself or others—and lean into these resources when you need them.

Consider author Ella Frances Sanders's words from her beautifully illustrated book, *Eating the Sun: Small Musings on a Vast Universe*:

> The carbon inside you, accounting for about 18 percent of your being, could have existed in any number of creatures or natural disasters before finding you. . . .
>
> You see, you are not so soft after all; you are rock and wave and the peeling bark of trees; you are ladybirds and the smell of a garden after the rain. When you put your best foot forward, you are taking the north side of a mountain with you.[15]

It's true. And even the most fractured, broken, and traumatized among us is no less a mountain or a star.

GROW TOWARD THE LIGHT

I have described what I term "the light of the future," the brilliant radiance of the Divine that pours into deep moments of spacious presence and illuminates profound new potentials for creativity and healing change. This is the *true* future, very different from the "tomorrows" we plan for but live out as mere repetitions of past patterns and unresolved yesterdays.

As all home gardeners will know, plants and flowers are heliotropic; they tend to grow in the direction of life-giving sunlight. Set a houseplant near a window and very soon its leaves and branches turn to face the incoming light. David L. Cooperrider, author and co-founder of the theory of Appreciative Inquiry, offers the "intriguing suggestion that human systems are largely 'heliotropic' in character, meaning that they exhibit an observable and largely automatic tendency to evolve in the direction of positive anticipatory images of the future."[16] According to Cooperrider, "Social systems evolve toward the most positive images they hold of themselves, toward what gives them life and energy." That's what the light of more true and beautiful futures offers to us. And we owe it to ourselves, to one another, and to the sacred planet we call home to face that light. To grow *toward* it.

Imagine what our world might start to look like if we did: a world in which our institutions, organizations, and natural ecosystems are expressions of resilience and balance. A world in which we practice collective intelligence and relational wisdom and in which we create fair, participatory, and well-balanced communities. A place where we respond readily and responsibly as parents, partners, leaders, and citizens. Where teachers, medical professionals, first responders, and others are supported and cared for, just as they support and care for their communities. A world in which we hold nature as sacred and we act to protect natural ecosystems and resources. Where we work to dispel scarcity and correct or repair economic and social imbalances, restoring each and every individual's honored place within the larger whole.

As we've explored throughout this book, attunement is the act of bringing more light—more consciousness, space, and presence in order to cohere relation and enhance or repair the self-healing function. Collective attunement is the act of bringing more light into the social field, to cohere the wider web of relations, and to restore balance to the great chain of increasingly complex human families, communities, cultures, and nations, perhaps fulfilling what Teilhard de Chardin described as "a system whose unity coincides with a paroxysm of harmonized complexity."[17]

That is the dazzling vision of humanity's future that I hold as a guiding light.

I have likewise described what I believe are our innate human rights: to be, to become, to belong. Of course, with these sacred rights come great responsibility—namely, the duty to act in alignment with the health of all beings. We are living in a time of astonishing upheaval and unimaginable promise. The profoundly complex challenges we face—intractable social problems, geopolitical conflicts, the existential threat of planetary climate change—demand a new level of human collaboration. Each of us has a chance to take part in this vital work, to bring our share of light and healing coherence to a struggling world. This work asks us to expand how we perceive and relate to the disruption and disorder, the residue of past trauma, within and around us—and to expand how we perceive and relate to one another. This moment is a holy opportunity to create more resilient communities and cultures that are strong *and* sensitive, hardy *and* flexible, curious *and* wise enough to meet global challenges head-on and act with a new level of concord and creativity to address them.

By upholding our sacred responsibility to integrate trauma, we, in effect, remove our shares from the collective trauma field, lessening the overall burden of suffering for others. This is not merely something some of us should do; it is work that all of us who are conscious and capable *must* do.

I beseech you to try.

Epilogue

Beyond any technique, relationships are what heal.
—LEWIS MEHL-MADRONA

Human beings are storytellers, which is to say we are meaning makers. The narratives we tell about who we are, where we come from, and the things that matter provide us with a rich sense of belonging, understanding, purpose, and direction. Trauma breaks open our stories. It erases the safety of old cultural narratives and damages our sense of shared identity, belonging, and purpose. This is how collective trauma produces a crisis of meaning.

Before the trauma, we knew who we were. We felt safe and connected and purposeful. After the trauma, we feel unmoored, disconnected, unsafe, and uncertain. To reclaim a sense of safety and purpose, we learn to reframe our cultural identity around the story of shared suffering and survival—and, perhaps, one day, around wholeness. As Gilad Hirschberger, professor of social and political psychology at Israel's Reichman University, writes:

> For victims, the memory of trauma may be adaptive for group survival, but it also elevates existential threat, which prompts a search for meaning, and the construction of a trans-generational collective self. For perpetrators, the memory of trauma poses a threat to collective identity that may be addressed by denying history, minimizing culpability for wrongdoing, transforming the memory of the event, closing the door on history, or accepting responsibility.[1]

Continuing to deny historical truths further annihilates survivor groups; it is a terrible retraumatization. But denial is also an unconscious agreement to cease or regress one's own growth and development. By accepting responsibility, perpetrators of collective trauma or their descendants break away from the conditioned narrative and ultimately disidentify with their former group self-concept. They find a renewed sense of group esteem as they retell their communal narratives with ownership, accountability, truth, and a sense of deeper understanding and inclusion. New meaning and purpose, along with new stories, are created from a position of responsibility to the traumatized, to the culture at large, and to one's own future descendants. As Hirschberger writes, "It is a process of identity construction that comprises the sense of self-esteem, continuity, distinctiveness, belonging, efficacy, and ultimately a sense of meaning."[2]

When we can feel ourselves in active relation with one another and with our natural environment, our minds become the instruments through which Spirit expresses Its beauty.

Trauma itself is a condition of absence—the absence of sufficient safety, support, resources, love. The absence of embodied relation. Thus, in times of trauma what is most needed is generosity, safety, presence, attunement, care, and embodied relation. These are the things that allow us to make meaning, new growth, and wisdom from our trauma. This wisdom brings with it the ability to more deeply attune and to hold more of the world within you, by which I mean the ability to stay related to the world inside you and to the one outside you. To hold another's worldspace within you is a deeply intimate and utterly relational act. Fundamentally, it is an expression of love. As we learn to hold more of the world—more of its messiness, its sadness, its confusion, its beauty—we grow in our uniquely divine capacity to love.

When we can feel ourselves in active relation with one another and with our natural environment, our minds become the instruments through which Spirit expresses Its beauty. And that is love, constantly occurring and always present. In this dynamic flow, we awaken to ourselves as luminous expressions of Life, and we feel—always as if for the first time—our innate intimacy with the sacred, timeless, and loving Presence embodied in a cosmos shimmering with consciousness. That, too, is love.

Love is at the center of it all. It is the root and heart, the foundation and the fire. It is the source of our deepest longing to connect and relate, to grow and to heal, to be and become and belong. These are the simplest, most essential ingredients of healing relation, and they are also its end product: the higher capacities afforded to us as a *result* of shared healing.

Love is at the center of it all.

I believe we are being called into a new era of healing work, in which we learn to connect personal healing work to the ancestral and collective map. This demands a global healing movement to address the complex, systemic nature of human and planetary suffering. To enact it, we must go to the root; we must learn to see ourselves as more than separate individuals, more than our tribal, political, or national identities. We must recognize our fundamental relationship of responsibility to other humans and to the natural world. We must awaken to the nature of our profound—and profoundly sacred—interdependence. *Not* to awaken is no longer an option; our very survival depends on it.

As civilization complexifies, the crises we face become ever more wicked, more intractable, and more dangerous. Yet, humankind has survived countless other eras of upending crisis and radical change. Our very bodies are encoded with the intelligence of countless generations, with the light of millions of years of life. So, no matter the challenges before us, I have every faith that we will rise to meet them.

May we awaken new pathways of attuned relation and healing integration. May we mature into a new story of being, becoming, and belonging. May we lean courageously into the scintillating light of our evolutionary future and find ourselves already, always whole.

Acknowledgments

This book could never have been realized without the hundreds of thousands of people who have bravely participated in, supported, and contributed to my work during the last twenty-plus years. To each, I offer my heartfelt gratitude. You have vitally shaped the work that is described in this book.

For everyone whose hard work and spirit of collaboration helped to midwife this book into being, I owe my sincerest thanks. Julie Jordan Avritt, thank you again for bringing your craft and refinement to the writing of this book; I am grateful for the unfolding richness of our collaboration. I also wish to thank Tami Simon for trusting my work and everyone at Sounds True who helped bring it to print, including Jennifer Brown, Sarah Stanton, Gretel Hakanson, Jade Lascelles, and Laurel Kallenbach, whose brilliant feedback helped to shine and polish the pages. I would also like to thank Lori Shridhare for her brilliant editorial insight and her selfless contribution to my work, and Amy Fox for her deep and heartfelt friendship, as much as for her collaboration and editorial support.

This book, in particular, and my work more broadly have been immeasurably enriched by the wisdom, insight, and many deep and inspiring conversations I've had with notable experts in the fields of trauma and human relationship. I offer my deepest thanks to Reverend angel Kyodo williams, Kamilah Majied, Ruby Mendenhall, Angel Acosta, and Karen Simms for their wisdom, guidance, and partnership in the work to address racial trauma and deepen diversity in our community. Their brilliance and generosity have been essential to the deepening of my work. I also wish to thank Eduardo Duran, Peter A. Levine, Gabor Maté, Stephen Porges, and Dan Siegel, whose expertise in the subject of trauma has shaped my thinking and my work. Thank you for the many brilliant conversations and for your generous participation in the annual Collective Trauma Summit.

I wish to also thank Kosha Joubert, CEO of The Pocket Project, and all the brilliant members of the staff and advisory panel who help to realize the organization's mission and vision. Your ongoing courage, commitment, and contribution to the research and understanding of collective trauma are vital ingredients toward the future of collective healing. My sincerest gratitude also goes to core team members Laura Calderón de la Barca, Hilorie Baer, Markus Hirzig, and Heidi Wohlhüter for their unique contribution in these pages and in the work we do together. Thank you also to the exceptional Ute Kostanjevec, Stacey Marvel, Claire Lanyado, Ami Singh, Karen Ben Baruch, Mathias Weitbrecht, Alli Brooks, and everyone working with Inner Science, LLC; Sharing the Presence, GmbH; and the Academy of Consciousness Evolution, Ltd. Your particular mastery and commitment are an invaluable contribution. My thanks also to the many mentors and assistants who have helped to produce the Timeless Wisdom Training.

I offer my gratitude to the memory of Terry Patten. May you rest in peace, my friend. And I owe a special debt of gratitude to my dear friend and spiritual mentor, David Ifergan, whose profound gifts for attunement and mystical wisdom run deep.

Finally, my deepest thanks to my wife, Yehudit Sasportas, and our daughter, Eliya, my greatest teachers in the arts of attunement, deep relation, and love.

Notes

INTRODUCTION

1. Joan Halifax, *The Fruitful Darkness: A Journey Through Buddhist Practice and Tribal Wisdom* (San Francisco: Harper Collins, 1993), xvi.
2. Radhika Deshmukh, et al., "Diverse Metabolic Capacities of Fungi for Bioremediation," *Indian Journal of Microbiology* 56, no. 3 (September 2016): 247–264.
3. Beatrice Bruteau, *God's Ecstasy: The Creation of a Self-Creating World* (New York: Crossroad, 1997).
4. Cynthia Bourgeault, *Personal Transformation and a New Creation: The Spiritual Revolution of Beatrice Bruteau*, ed. Ilia Delio (Maryknoll, NY: Orbis Books, 2016), 77–78.
5. Hildegard of Bingen, *Meditations with Hildegard of Bingen*, ed. Gabriele Uhlein (Santa Fe, NM: Bear & Company, 1982), 41.
6. Thomas Berry, *Evening Thoughts: Reflecting on Earth as a Sacred Community* (Berkeley, CA: Counterpoint, 2015), 17–18.
7. Brigid Brophy, *Black & White: A Portrait of Aubrey Beardsley* (New York: Stein and Day, 1969).

CHAPTER 1: ANCIENT PRINCIPLES, EVOLUTIONARY INSIGHTS

1. Manjit Kumar, *Quantum: Einstein, Bohr, and the Great Debate about the Nature of Reality* (London: Icon Books, 2014), 312.

2. Robert Lanza with Bob Berman, *Biocentrism: How Life and Consciousness Are the Keys to Understanding the True Nature of the Universe* (Dallas, TX: BenBella Books, 2010).

3. Malcolm W. Browne, "Far Apart, Two Particles Respond Faster than Light," *The New York Times*, July 22, 1997: C, 1.

4. F. Fröwis, P. C., Strassmann, A. Tiranov, et al., "Experimental certification of millions of genuinely entangled atoms in a solid," *Nature Communications* 8, no. 907 (2017): 1.

5. Mark DeWolfe Howe, ed., *Holmes-Pollock Letters: The Correspondence of Mr. Justice Holmes and Sir Frederick Pollock, 1874–1932* (Cambridge, MA: Harvard University Press, 2nd ed., 1961), 109.

6. Jean Gebser, *The Ever-Present Origin, Part One: Foundations of the Aperspectival World and Part Two: Manifestations of the Aperspectival World,* trans. Algis Mickunas and Noel Barstad (Athens, OH: Ohio University Press, 2020).

7. David A. Kunin, *Kaddish* (New York: New Paradigm Matrix, 2016), 384.

CHAPTER 2: ESSENTIAL PRINCIPLES OF HUMAN DEVELOPMENT

1. Peter Levine, *Trauma and Memory: Brain and Body in a Search for the Living Past* (Berkeley, CA: North Atlantic Books, 2015), 74–94.

2. Katherine Gould, "The Vagus Nerve: Your Body's Information Superhighway," *LiveScience* (Nov 12, 2019), accessed January 2020, tinyurl.com/tbdchcg.

3. Sarah Beutler, et al. "Trauma-related dissociation and the autonomic nervous system: a systematic literature review of psychophysiological correlates of dissociative experiencing in PTSD patients" *European Journal of Psychotraumatology* 13:2 (November 2022), doi: 10.1080/20008066.2022.2132599.

4. Stephen W. Porges, "The polyvagal perspective," *Biological Psychology* 74, no. 2 (Feb 2007): 116–143.

5. "Tend-and-befriend response," *APA Dictionary of Psychology*, American Psychological Association (2018), accessed January 2020, tinyurl.com/thkyqwh.

6. George Santayana, *Reason in Common Sense: The Life of Reason, Volume 1* (Mineola, NY: Dover Publications, 1980).

CHAPTER 3: THE ART OF ATTUNEMENT

1. Daniel J. Siegel, *Mindsight: The New Science of Personal Transformation* (New York: Bantam Books, 2010), 10, 27.

2. Jini Patel Thompson, "Hawks vs. Horses for Human Therapy & Energy Training," YouTube video, 35:01, published 10 Nov 2019, youtube.com/watch?v=jfJ7aRqZJKg.

CHAPTER 4: THE ART OF TRANSPARENT COMMUNICATION

1. Rupert Sheldrake, *Dogs That Know When Their Owners Are Coming Home* (New York: Random House, 1999), 303.

2. John Hogan, "Scientific Heretic Rupert Sheldrake on Morphic Fields, Psychic Dogs, and Other Mysteries," *Scientific American* blog (July 2014), tinyurl.com/ybsknytg.

3. Peter Senge, Otto Scharmer, Joseph Jaworski, Betty Sue Flowers, "Awakening Faith in an Alternative Future," *Reflections: Society for Organizational Learning Journal* 5, no. 7 (2004), 3.

4. Robin Wall Kimmerer, *Gathering Moss: A Natural and Cultural History of Mosses* (Corvallis, OR: Oregon State University Press, 2003), 11.

5. Cynthia Bourgeault, *Personal Transformation and a New Creation: The Spiritual Revolution of Beatrice Bruteau*, ed. Ilia Delio (Maryknoll, NY: Orbis Books, 2016), 85.

6. Sheldrake, *Dogs That Know*, 24.

7. Robert Lanza, *Beyond Biocentrism: Rethinking Time, Space, Consciousness, and the Illusion of Death* (Dallas, TX: BenBella Books, 2016), 153, 73.

8. Richard Tarnas, *Cosmos and Psyche: Intimations of a New World View* (New York: Viking/Penguin Group, 2006), 448.

CHAPTER 5: PRESENCING THE SHADOW

1. Christopher Uhl, *Developing Ecological Consciousness* (Washington, DC: Rowman and Littlefield Publishers, 2013), 206.

2. Edward Edinger, *Transformation of the God-Image: An Elucidation of Jung's Answer to Job* (Scarborough, ON: Inner City Books, 1992), 70–71.

3. Marcie Boucouvalas, *Creativity, Spirituality, and Transcendence: Paths to Integrity and Wisdom in the Mature Self*, eds. Melvin Miller and Susanne Cook-Greuter (Stamford, CT: Ablex Publishing, 2000), 210.

4. Beena Sharma, "Midwifing the New Unity," UnityLeaders.org (March 2013), accessed August 2020, tinyurl.com/y3hd3tuh.

5. "Embodied Cognition," *Stanford Encyclopedia of Philosophy* (June 2011), accessed July 2021, tinyurl.com/zpj4ck4d.

6. Ana Lucía Valencia and Tom Froese, "What binds us? Inter-brain neural synchronization and its implications for theories of human consciousness," *Neuroscience of Consciousness* 6, no. 1 (2020), doi: 10.1093/nc/niaa010.

7. Jorge Ferrer, *Revisioning Transpersonal Theory: A Participatory Vision of Human Spirituality* (Albany, NY: State University of New York Press, 2002), 2–3.

CHAPTER 6: TRAUMA'S IMPACT

1. Janna Levin, *Black Hole Survival Guide* (New York: Knopf, 2020), 5.

2. The number of men, women, and children in Primo Levi's transport from Italy to Auschwitz who survived is unclear. Some sources claim Levi was only one of three; most estimate twenty. Berel Lang, author of *Primo Levi: The Matter of a Life* (New Haven, CT: Yale University Press, 2013), says twenty-four survived.

3. Primo Levi, *The Reawakening*, trans. Stuart Woolf (London: The Bodley Head, 1965), 207.

4. Elie Wiesel, "Con l'incubo che tutto sia accaduto invano" ["With the nightmare that it all happened in vain"], *La Stampa* Turin, April 14, 1987, 3.

5. William Faulkner, *Requiem for a Nun* (New York: Vintage Books, 1951), 73.

6. "What Is Psychological Trauma?" Penn Center for Trauma Response and Recovery, Perelman School of Medicine, University of Pennsylvania, accessed February 16, 2023, mentalhealth.cityofnewyork.us/wp-content/uploads/2021/04 /033121-TraumaSupport-Guide-FINAL.pdf.

7. Peter A. Levine, *Healing Trauma: A Pioneering Program for Restoring the Wisdom of Your Body* (Boulder, CO: Sounds True, 2008), 2.

8. Peter Levine, *Healing Trauma*, 13.

9. "Child Trauma Effects," The National Child Traumatic Stress Network, accessed January 1, 2020, tinyurl.com/yanccf5n.

10. Clara Mucci, *Beyond Individual and Collective Trauma: Intergenerational Transmission, Psychoanalytic Treatment, and the Dynamics of Forgiveness* (New York: Routledge, 2013), 2.

11. Werner Bohleber, "Remembrance, trauma, and collective memory: The battle for memory in psychoanalysis," *The International Journal of Psychoanalysis* 88, no. 2 (2007): 335.

12. "ACEs and Toxic Stress," Harvard University Center on the Developing Child, accessed December 2020, tinyurl.com /y7nm7ajj.

13. "ACEs and Toxic Stress."

14. Maria Yellow Horse Brave Heart, "The historical trauma response among natives and its relationship with substance abuse: a Lakota illustration," *Journal of Psychoactive Drugs* 35, no. 1 (January–March 2003): 7.

15. Helen Epstein, *Children of the Holocaust: Conversations with Sons and Daughters of Survivors* (New York: Penguin, 1988), 185–90.

16. Martha Henriques, "Can the Legacy of Trauma Be Passed Down the Generations?" *BBC Future*, March 26, 2019, BBC .com/future/article/20190326-what-is-epigenetics.

17. Henriques, "Can the Legacy of Trauma Be Passed Down?"

18. Exodus 34: 6–7 (King James Version).

19. Bessel van der Kolk, Alexander McFarlane, and Lars Weisaeth, *Traumatic Stress: The Effects of Overwhelming Experience on Mind, Body, and Society* (New York: Guilford Press, 1996), 4.

20. Cathy Caruth, ed., *Trauma: Explorations in Memory* (Baltimore, MD: Johns Hopkins University Press, 1995), 11.

21. This is an excerpt from an interview with Hilorie Baer, conducted by Julie Jordan Avritt in November 2021 on the topic of ancestral trauma.

22. Clara Mucci, *Beyond Individual and Collective Trauma* (New York: Routledge, 2013), 4.

23. Kai T. Erickson, *Everything in Its Path: Destruction of Community in the Buffalo Creek Flood* (New York: Simon & Schuster, 1976), 154.

24. George Musser, "The Most Famous Paradox in Physics Nears Its End," *Quanta Magazine*, October 29, 2020, accessed January 1, 2021, tinyurl.com/yxdcoscf.

CHAPTER 7: THE POWER OF HEALING RELATION

1. Lao Tzu, *Tao Te Ching*, trans. Stephen Mitchell (New York: HarperPerennial, 1988), 63.
2. Daniel Siegel, *Mindsight* (New York: Bantam, 2010), 9–10.
3. Introduction to *Multisystemic Resilience,* ed. Michael Ungar (Oxford University Press, 2001), 1.
4. Richard Tedeschi and Lawrence Calhoun, "Posttraumatic Growth: Conceptual Foundations and Empirical Evidence," *Psychological Inquiry* 15, no. 1 (2004): 1–18.
5. Tzu, *Tao Te Ching*, 25.

CHAPTER 8: GUIDANCE FOR FACILITATORS OF HEALING

1. Andreas Weber, "Skincentric Ecology," *Minding Nature* 14, no. 1 (Spring 2021), humansandnature.org/skincentric-ecology.
2. Andrew Garner and Michael Yogman, "Preventing Childhood Toxic Stress: Partnering with Families and Communities to Promote Relational Health," Policy Statement, *American Academy of Pediatrics* 148, no. 2 (2021).
3. Garner and Yogman, "Preventing Childhood Toxic Stress."
4. *The Surgeon's Cut: Saving Life Before Birth*, directed by Andrew Cohen and James Van der Pool, BBC Studios for Netflix, 2020.
5. My book on the latter category, *Healing Collective Trauma: A Process for Integrating Our Intergenerational and Cultural Wounds,* was published by Sounds True in 2020, so I will only briefly cover the concepts of that work in this chapter.
6. Dr. Gabor Maté was featured in the film, *The Wisdom of Trauma,* directed by Zaya and Maurizio Benazzo, Science & Nonduality (2021), 16:18 min.
7. J. F. Le Goff, "Boszormenyi-Nagy and Contextual Therapy: An Overview," *The Australian and New Zealand Journal of Family Therapy* 22, no. 3 (2001): 147–57.

8. Arnold Mindell, *River's Way: The Process Science of the Dreambody* (Portland, OR: Deep Democracy Exchange, 2011), 11.

9. Joy Harjo, *Poet Warrior: A Memoir* (New York: W. W. Norton & Company, 2021), 20.

10. Harjo, *Poet Warrior*, 53.

CHAPTER 9: ANCESTRAL HEALING

1. Birago Diop, "Spirits," in *The Negritude Poets: An Anthology of Translations from the French,* ed., trans. Ellen Conroy Kennedy (New York: Viking Press, 1975), 152–4.

2. Daniel Foor, *Ancestral Medicine: Rituals for Personal and Family Healing* (Rochester, VT: Bear & Company, 2017), 21.

3. Ewen Callaway, "Fearful memories haunt mouse descendants," *Nature*, December 1, 2013, nature.com/articles/nature.

4. From "An Indigenous Lens on Psychotherapy as a Soul Healing," a talk by Dr. Eduardo Duran in October 2021 at the Collective Trauma Summit 2021: Collective Healing in Action.

5. Harville Hendrix, *Getting the Love You Want: A Guide for Couples* (New York: Henry Holt & Company, 1988).

CHAPTER 10: HEALING FOR THE COLLECTIVE

1. Jamey Keaten, "UN: 6.5 million people displaced inside Ukraine due to war," *Associated Press News*, March 18, 2022, accessed March 21, 2022, tinyurl.com/26yk3497.

2. "Figures at a Glance," UNHCR: The UN Refugee Agency, accessed March 2022, unhcr.org/en-us/figures-at-a-glance.html.

3. "About Refugees," The National Child Traumatic Stress Network (NCTSN), accessed March 2022, tinyurl.com/mv7jafu2.

4. "Five Facts on Climate Migrants," United Nations University: Institute for Environment and Human Security, 2015, accessed March 2022, tinyurl.com/3x7wawxt.

5. Thomas Moore, "A Dark Night of the Soul and the Discovery of Meaning," *Kosmos Quarterly* (Spring/Summer 2015), tinyurl.com/mr3dh76k.

6. The term *Holodomor* derives from the Ukrainian words for hunger, *holod*, and extermination, *mor*.

7. Anne Applebaum, *Red Famine: Stalin's War on Ukraine* (New York: Doubleday, 2017).

8. Andrea Graziosi, "The Soviet 1931–1933 Famines and the Ukrainian Holodomor: Is a New Interpretation Possible, and What Would Its Consequences Be?" *Harvard Ukrainian Studies* 27, nos. 1–4: 97–115.

9. Samantha Marriage and Keith Marriage, "Too Many Sad Stories: Clinician Stress and Coping," *The Canadian Child and Adolescent Psychiatric Review* (November 2005) 14, no. 4 (November 2005): 114–117.

10. Luke Munn, "Angry by Design: Toxic Communication and Digital Architectures," *Humanities and Social Sciences Communications* 7, no. 53 (2020), doi.org/10.1057/s41599-020-00550-7.

11. David Seamon and Arthur Zajonc, eds., *Goethe's Way of Science: A Phenomenology of Nature* (Albany, NY: State University of New York Press, 1998), 257.

12. Gordon Wells, *Dialogic Inquiry: Towards a Sociocultural Practice and Theory of Education* (Cambridge, UK: Cambridge University Press, 1999), vii.

13. Gus Speth, *Practicing Sustainability*, ed. Guruprasad Madhavan et al. (New York: Springer Science & Business Media, 2012).

14. I describe the Collective Trauma Integration Process more in-depth in *Healing Collective Trauma*.

15. Ella Frances Sanders, *Eating the Sun: Small Musings on a Vast Universe* (New York: Penguin Books, 2019).

16. David L. Cooperrider, "Positive Image, Positive Action: The Affirmative Basis of Organizing," *Appreciative Management and Leadership: The Power of Positive Thought and Action in Organization* (New York: Crown Cover Publishing, 1999), 2.

17. Teilhard de Chardin, *The Phenomenon of Man*, trans. Bernard Wall (New York: Harper Perennial, 1959 and 2002), 262.

EPILOGUE

1. Gilad Hirschberger, "Collective Trauma and the Social Construction of Meaning," *Frontiers in Psychology* 9 (August 2018): 1441, doi.org/10.3389/fpsyg.2018.01441.

2. Hirschberger, "Collective Trauma and the Social Construction of Meaning."

Resources

Below is a condensed list of publications, media, and courses (online and in person) that readers of *Attuned* may find helpful.

WORKS BY THOMAS HÜBL

Hübl, Thomas, with Julie Jordan Avritt. *Healing Collective Trauma: A Process for Integrating Our Intergenerational and Collective Wounds.* Boulder, CO: Sounds True, 2020.

Hübl, Thomas. *The Power of We: Awakening in the Relational Field.* Boulder, CO: Sounds True, 2014. Audio CD.

Hübl, Thomas. Introduction to Global Social Witnessing. The Pocket Project, 2022. Video, 55:23 min. This video introduction to Thomas Hübl's Global Social Witnessing practice is available at pocketproject.org/videos/global-social-witnessing-introduction-mindfully-attending-the-world/.

Hübl, Thomas, and Lori Shridhare. "The 'Tender Narrator' Who Sees Beyond Time: A Framework for Trauma Integration and Healing." *Journal of Awareness-Based Systems Change* 2(2) (November 2022). doi.org/10.47061/jasc.v2i2.4937. In this article, reference is made to the "tender narrator" as an exploratory framework for understanding the role of narrative in voicing trauma as part of the healing process, specifically in group settings.

Shridhare, Lori. "Collective Action for Collective Healing" (Q&A with Thomas Hübl). *The Harvard Gazette* (December 3, 2020). In this interview, Hübl addresses community and world traumas—and how to repair them. news.harvard.edu/gazette/story/2020/12/moving-from-individual-to-collective-healing/.

OTHER RESEARCH

These bibliographic references point to some of the important authors and researchers whose work informed the writing of this book. I bow to their genius.

Matoba, Kazuma. (2021). "Global Social Witnessing: An Educational Tool for Awareness-Based Systems Change in the Era of Global Humanitarian and Planetary Crisis." *Journal of Awareness-Based Systems Change* 1(1), 59–74. doi.org/10.47061/jabsc.v1i1.548.

Matoba, Kazuma. "'Measuring' Collective Trauma: A Quantum Social Science Approach." *Integrative Psychological and Behavioral Science* (April 30, 2022). doi.org/10.1007/s12124-022-09696-2.

Mollica, Richard F., and Thomas Hübl. "Numb from the news? Understanding why and what to do may help." *Harvard Health* (March 18, 2021). Dr. Richard Mollica, professor of psychiatry at Harvard Medical School, is a pioneer in international research on refugee trauma. He's also director of the Harvard Program in Refugee Trauma (HPRT) at Massachusetts General Hospital. health.harvard.edu/blog/numb-from-the-news-understanding-why-and-what-to-do-may-help-2021031822176.

STUDY WITH THOMAS

To learn about online courses, practice groups, graduate degree programs, and more, please visit:

thomashuebl.com

pocketproject.org

timelesswisdomtraining.com

For more resources and for a list of certified ITIP, ATIP, and CTIP trainers and facilitators, please write to Thomas Hübl at thomashuebl. com/contact. Listen to recordings of Thomas guiding the meditation practices in the book at attunedbook.com.

About the Author

Thomas Hübl is a renowned teacher, international facilitator, and author of *Healing Collective Trauma: A Process for Integrating Our Intergenerational and Cultural Wounds* (Sounds True, 2020), whose work seeks to integrate the core insights of the great wisdom traditions with the discoveries of contemporary science.

Originally a paramedic for nine years and a student of medicine for four, Hübl left his studies at the University of Vienna to spend four years on retreat. This led to a new life path focused on teaching meditation and mindfulness-based awareness practices.

Since the early 2000s, Hübl has taught courses, led international workshops, and facilitated large-scale healing retreats designed to address humanity's most painful atrocities and unhealed collective traumas. By leading large-group change processes, Hübl developed the Collective Trauma Integration Process (CTIP), a model that promotes safe sharing and reflection and supports radical openness, transparent communication, mindful awareness, and refined relational competencies. With his wife, Yehudit Sasportas, he co-founded The Pocket Project, a nonprofit organization with the mission to support research and the healing of collective trauma throughout the world.

Hübl's large-scale events have brought together thousands of Germans and Jewish people from around the world to acknowledge, face, and heal the cultural shadow left by the Holocaust. And in the last decade, his events—held in the United States, Israel, Germany, Spain, Argentina, and elsewhere—have focused on processing the mass traumatization brought about by racism, oppression, colonialism, genocide, gender violence, the climate crisis, and other historic and contemporary challenges.

Since 2019, Hübl has hosted the annual Collective Trauma Summit, which has brought together more than one hundred speakers and 350,000 participants from more than 120 countries. He leads workshops and training programs at Harvard Medical School, the California Institute of Integral Studies, the Mobius Institute, Ubiquity University, the Science and Nonduality Conference, and the Garrison Institute.

His organization, the Academy of Inner Science (founded in 2008), has launched master's and doctoral studies programs in cooperation with universities in Europe and the United States. Hübl received a PhD in Wisdom Studies from Ubiquity University in 2022.

The interdisciplinary nature of Hübl's work is practiced by working groups and partnerships with physicians, psychologists, and therapists from the United States, Germany, Israel, Canada, and other countries. These professionals have trained under his tutelage to learn competencies that support their patients and clients, while they work to make health care more innovative, empathic, and trauma informed.

As a coach and advisor, Hübl serves senior leaders of global organizations, consulting companies, and government organizations. He regularly trains therapists, coaches, mediators, and facilitators, and he provides ongoing supervision for these groups. If you're interested in learning more about these services or would like a list of trained therapists and facilitators, please reach out by using the contact page at thomashuebl.com.

A native of Austria, Hübl resides in Tel Aviv, Israel, with his wife, award-winning Israeli artist and teacher Yehudit Sasportas, and their daughter, Eliya.

About the Co-author

Julie Jordan Avritt is a professional ghostwriter, collaborator, book coach, and integral thinker working with global changemakers, cultural upstarts, and renegades on a mission to inspire humanity in a time of great transition. Her clients publish at the intersection of science and spirituality and have produced work on the *New York Times* and *Washington Post* bestseller lists.

She lives in southern Appalachia with her daughter, Journey, and two feline familiars, Truman Catpote and Esther, Destroyer of Worlds.

About Sounds True

Sounds True was founded in 1985 by Tami Simon with a clear mission: to disseminate spiritual wisdom. Since starting out as a project with one woman and her tape recorder, we have grown into a multimedia publishing company with a catalog of more than 3,000 titles by some of the leading teachers and visionaries of our time, and an ever-expanding family of beloved customers from across the world.

In more than three decades of evolution, Sounds True has maintained our focus on our overriding purpose and mission: to wake up the world. We offer books, audio programs, online learning experiences, and in-person events to support your personal growth and awakening, and to unlock our greatest human capacities to love and serve.

At SoundsTrue.com you'll find a wealth of resources to enrich your journey, including our weekly Insights at the Edge podcast, free downloads, and information about our nonprofit Sounds True Foundation, where we strive to remove financial barriers to the materials we publish through scholarships and donations worldwide.

To learn more, please visit SoundsTrue.com/freegifts or call us toll-free at 800.333.9185.

Together, we can wake up the world.

sounds true
WAKING UP THE WORLD